No matter how the journey of life would unfold for the family of Jordan and Charlotte Holiday, the spirit of Christmas would remain forever constant, representing what it should have represented from the beginning: Hope in the face of despair. Life in the face of death. And light in the face of impenetrable darkness. From now on, every Christmas morning would begin with a glorious sunrise. And every Christmas Day would be accompanied by a song on the wind that spoke of things more beautiful than the eye could see and more wonderful than the ear could hear. . . .

A RETURN
TO
CHRISTMAS

Chris Heimerdinger

IVY BOOKS • NEW YORK

An Ivy Book
Published by The Ballantine Publishing Group
Copyright © 1996 by Chris Heimerdinger

Ivy Books and colophon are trademarks of Random House, Inc.

www.randomhouse.com/BB/

Library of Congress Catalog Card Number: 99-90739

ISBN 0-8041-1826-4

Manufactured in the United States of America

First Ballantine Hardcover Edition: October 1997
First Ballantine Mass Market Edition: November 1999

10 9 8 7 6 5 4 3 2 1

For Matthew

And for his rescuers, his new parents,
Michael and Jeannette Watson

One

ARTEMUS WATCHED CHEERLESSLY as the snowflakes landed one by one on the windshield of his father's Lexus LS 400. Each flake would pause there momentarily, a perfect little six-pointed creation. That is, until the heated interior of the car melted the icy speck into a water droplet that weaved its way down the glass. Typical, he thought, of the fate of all perfect things.

His fourth-grade teacher, Mrs. Livermore, had once told him that no two snowflakes were exactly alike. According to her, of all the hundreds of flakes that now fell upon his windshield, as well as the thousands that fell upon the dead grass of the cemetery, or even the billions that fell upon every mountain and field of the world year after year, no single pair was exactly the same.

CHRIS HEIMERDINGER

Hogwash, thought Artemus. Who on earth had actually gone to the trouble to compare enough snowflakes to really know for sure? Who'd even gone so far as to compare the total number in one snowdrift along one hillside after a single snowstorm? How could anybody *possibly* know if somewhere in Siberia there hadn't fallen a snowflake that looked exactly like the one now melting on the glass?

He focused beyond the windshield and saw his mother and father, as well as his sister, Amber, still gathered at the tombstone. It was a tall monument, pure marble—no less than the best for the son of Jordan and Charlotte Holiday. From where Artemus sat, he could just read the words on the plaque—ANDREW CHESTER HOLIDAY, BORN DECEMBER 20, 1984, DIED DECEMBER 25, 1987. Andrew had been three years old. Exactly three years and five days.

His mother neatly arranged gardenia flowers at the base of the pedestal. *When I die,* thought Artemus, *I hope nobody puts gardenias on my grave.* The silky white petals were way too girlish. He wondered if his twin brother Andrew would have felt the same. That is, if he had lived.

His father and mother chose gardenias for a reason. Once, when Andrew was two and a half, he'd laid claim to a gardenia corsage that his mother had worn at a banquet. For two days he'd carried the fragile bloom everywhere he went, burying his nose

2

in its waxy whiteness. When the petals finally browned and fell away, Andrew's heart was broken. With a tear in his eye, he handed the entire mess to his mother, saying, "Fix, Mommy. Fix."

But Charlotte couldn't fix it. Nor could she bring back her little son, gone forever at the age of three, his small body resting in a tiny coffin beneath the dark soil of a Salt Lake City cemetery. Never again would she hold him or kiss him or sing him to sleep with a lullaby. After Andrew's death, Charlotte vowed that her son would never be long without the sweet smell of his favorite flower. Every fourth Sunday for the last eight years, she'd faithfully placed a white gardenia at the base of the memorial. She hadn't missed a single month.

But today wasn't Sunday. It was Wednesday, December 20—Andrew's birthday. Today he would have been eleven years old. In consequence of this, the number of gardenias adorning the pedestal's base was eleven.

The flowers had cost over a hundred and fifty dollars. But Artemus realized that such an expense was no great sacrifice for his parents. His father had made his fortune designing software for the banking industry. But despite living in a comfortable house on Salt Lake's east beaches, and despite enjoying many other trappings of financial success, Artemus would not have described his family as happy. Especially now that winter had come again. Now that the neighborhoods glittered with colorful strings of lights. Now that the songs of the season jammed the airwaves. Now that the memories of that terrible day could be most vividly recalled.

Artemus hated this time of year. For eight years, he'd known it only as the anniversary of the day his best friend had left him. Every other memory from his first three years of life had faded. But the image of Andrew remained. The two of them had been inseparable, sharing a magical connection that only twins can understand. When Andrew laughed, Artemus laughed. When he cried, Artemus cried too. For years, Artemus was bitter that his brother had left him behind.

When Andrew died, Artemus lost more than a brother. He lost Christmas itself. And every other day on the December calendar. For the last eight years—which pretty much comprised his entire life—all he could recall about December was that it was a month shrouded by gloom and depression and sojourns to the cemetery. Yes, he hated this time of year. He hated it with a passion.

On the radio, he heard the first chords of "O Little Town of Bethlehem." He was about to reach over and change the station when he noticed his sister, Amber, heading back to the car. Amber was two years older than Artemus, and she made it a point to remind him of this at every opportunity. His parents remained at the memorial for a few moments alone. Mom had buried her face in Dad's shoulder. It was a common scene. Artemus looked away, overcome by a familiar urge. If only he could escape. Run somewhere. Leave this city, this state, this *family* for good, and find a place where pain and guilt and terrible memories were not allowed and could never follow him.

Amber hopped into the backseat and closed the door. "I hope you know," she scolded, "you hurt Mom and Dad's feelings. Was it asking so much for you to stay and help arrange the gardenias?"

Artemus let this smolder for a moment. Finally he said, almost under his breath, "Everyone seems to forget. Today is *my* birthday too."

He changed the station to rock and roll.

Two

ELEVEN-YEAR-OLD CHESS FOLSOM crouched behind the garbage Dumpster at the edge of the park. For several minutes, he'd been watching the stranger who sat on the park bench directly in front of the swings. He didn't like what he saw. The man smugly read a newspaper, while his small daughter played alone on the slide. He'd overheard the daughter ask him to push her in the swing. "In a minute," he'd replied, not looking up.

She'd gone down the slide twelve times now. Her father wasn't even watching. Now and then she'd glance up at him to see if there was any change, any recognition, any attention. There was nothing.

Chess shook his head. Such a display was all he needed to justify what was about to happen.

At last, Uncle Boone appeared at the other end of the park. In his hands was a tiny green velvet box. Boone approached the playground area. Some snowflakes had fallen earlier, and the sky threatened more. This left only a handful of people in the park. But Chess knew from experience that it was better this way. He watched Boone move from person to person, making his way toward the stranger on the bench. Chess strained to hear him converse with the various people. Not that it was necessary to hear. He'd observed his uncle in action so many times that he could have read his lips. "Have you run across my diamond engagement ring?" he'd inquire, his voice on edge with desperation. "Or maybe your kids? I was here with my fiancée earlier today, and somehow I misplaced it."

The people would shake their heads, express concern, and ask for more details. Boone described the ring and offered a substantial reward for its recovery. He presented his business card and scribbled a local phone number where he could be reached. Children began scouring the sand and grass. Sometimes the grown-ups would also look, but Chess knew that for most adults, crawling around on your hands and knees was too undignified, even for a substantial reward.

Boone had made it a point to approach people within hearing range of the actual target—the man

7

reading the newspaper. Then, at last, he approached the mark.

"Excuse me," said Boone.

The man lowered his paper, although Chess had caught him looking up several times to eavesdrop.

Boone continued. "I'm sorry to bother you, but have you seen—"

The man interrupted. "I heard. Where were you when the ring was lost?"

"Actually, I was sitting on this bench," said Boone. "But I think I lost it before that. I've looked everywhere. There are rubies around the diamond setting and etchings on the band. I'm offering a $750 reward."

"Must be an expensive ring," said the man.

Boone pretended indifference, making it even more obvious that the man's assessment was correct. He wrote a local number on a business card. "This is my address in Florida, but I'll be staying at this number for the next couple days. If you or your kids happen to run across it, please, *please* call me. I'm desperate."

He'd played his part flawlessly, as usual. The man looked up occasionally as Boone made his way to the other end of the park. At last, Boone disappeared behind a stand of trees. The stranger's eyes surveyed the grass under the bench, but only once. He returned to his newspaper, convinced that the odds of finding the ring were too astronomical, especially since the owner himself had failed.

His daughter requested another push in the swing. He deflected her by suggesting that she look around for "that man's ring." Disappointed, she returned to the slide.

It was time for Chess to move in.

The situation with the girl gave him an idea. Normally, his success rate was about fifty-fifty. The little girl might improve his odds. He approached casually, like any eleven-year-old, even noisily kicking a Dr Pepper can part of the way. When he reached the playground, he climbed to the top of the slide. The girl was there already, not particularly anxious to go down. Chess's appearance reminded her to go, and he slid down after her.

At the bottom he asked, "Would you like to swing? I'll push."

Her face lit up.

Chess encouraged her to sit in the swing directly in front of her father. "He's gonna push me, Daddy," said the little girl.

"That's real nice of him." The man smiled at Chess, grateful that he could now finish his sports page uninterrupted.

"I have a little sister," Chess told the man, and then his face went gravely somber. "That is . . . I used to." He turned away slowly and started pushing the

9

swing, wondering if that last statement had pressed his luck. Better ease off.

The fact was, Chess couldn't have said for certain whether he had a sister or not. He wasn't even sure he had a father, although biology sort of made that obvious. He'd never known his real father, and he had only a fleeting memory of his mother. His life had been spent with various foster families, most of whom had given him back to the state after a couple of weeks. They labeled him a "behavioral challenge." To Chess this meant one thing: he was too difficult to love.

His only known relative was Boone Folsom, a fact that he'd discovered after snitching his case file. But Boone was a drifter and had a long criminal record—not a good candidate for becoming a foster parent. Eighteen months ago, Chess had run away from a halfway house in Tallahassee. After a two-week adventure hitching rides and eating only what he could steal, he finally hooked up with his uncle in a boarding house in Jacksonville.

Boone wasn't the most personable fellow Chess had ever met. In fact, he could be downright vicious. He'd seen his uncle do some terrible things. Unmentionable things. But Chess did his best to block this out. As far as he could tell, life was just one terrible thing after another anyway. Most important, Boone was *family*. That word carried a sacred resonance for Chess. Boone was also the first person who'd ever taught him anything really useful. He'd also credited his uncle for giving him his nickname—"Chess"—which was tons better than his real name—*Lawrence*.

"Higher!" the little girl yelled. "Higher!" Chess pushed her higher.

The father began folding his newspaper. "All right, Princess. Thank the boy, and let's get going."

Time to strike, thought Chess.

"Hey," he said to the girl after stopping the swing. "Wanna see something pretty?"

"Okay," she agreed.

Chess reached into his pocket and pulled out what appeared to be a gold ring with a very large diamond and several rubies around the setting. The girl gave a long "oooh."

The father approached. "Where'd you get that, son?"

"Found it," said Chess. "Over by that Dumpster. It was just layin' in the grass."

"May I see it?"

Chess closed his fist tightly around the ring and moved back a step, shaking his head. "I found it. I think it may be real. I'm gonna show it to my brother and see if we can sell it."

"Weren't you here when that man came by looking for that?"

11

"Looking for *this*? I don't think so. This one is *mine*."

"He was offering a reward."

Chess's expression changed. "Oh yeah? How much?"

The man stumbled a little as he said, "Fifty dollars."

"Fifty bucks! Really? Where is he?" Chess looked eagerly up and down the park.

"He's gone now," said the man. "But I happen to know how to get in touch with him. You see, he's a friend."

"He is? And he's offering fifty dollars for *this*?"

"I'll tell you what," said the man. "I'll give you fifty dollars for it right now. Then I'll get him to pay me."

Chess bit the inside of his cheeks. "Mmmm, I don't know. If this is real, it's probably worth a lot more than fifty dollars."

The man grew impatient. He stepped toward him. Chess moved back even farther, ready to run if necessary. He was certain he could outrun this clod. He and his uncle always kept this in mind when they selected a mark.

The man relented. "All right, listen. I'll give you a hundred for it. I'm sure he'd pay a hundred if I told him the circumstances."

Chess chewed on this. "You're really gonna give me a hundred dollars for this?"

The man reached for his wallet. He began counting out twenties and tens. He came up short. "I only got seventy, kid. Is it a deal?"

"You said a hundred."

The man became frustrated. "I don't *have* a hundred. What if I wrote you a check? You could have your dad help you cash it."

With a lame offer like that, Chess lost all fear of being assaulted. He'd been cautious ever since Des Moines, when the mark had grabbed him, pried open his fingers, and smacked him across the face.

He looked at the money, then back at the stranger. "If I tell you where I live, will you bring me the rest later?"

The man grinned. "Sure thing. Just tell me where you live." He held out the bills.

Chess snatched them away and dropped the ring into his palm. "I live down that street," he said. "Second house on the left." He stuffed the cash into his pocket as he ran.

Five minutes later, Chess met up with Boone at the designated place—the parking lot in front of the Tracy Aviary. Boone had their 1982 Buick Skylark running and ready. Chess hopped inside.

"What happened?" he asked, pulling out of the stall.

"No sweat," said Chess. "He's probably at a pay phone right now, trying to call that phony number."

He pulled the money out of his pocket. "Seventy bucks."

"Seventy!" Boone reached over and popped Chess hard on the ear. "What did I tell you? I said no less than a *hundred*!" He yanked the bills away.

Chess cringed and held his bruised ear. "He didn't *have* a hundred!"

"When I tell you to get a hundred, boy, you better darn well get a hundred!"

"The ring only cost us two bucks to begin with. What was I 'sposed to do? Take a check?"

"If he offered it, you shoulda taken it."

"But you always say the faster you close and get out of there—"

"Don't you get it, Chess? We're *broke*! And we only got four rings left."

Chess frowned. "But last night we still had three hundred dollars. What happened—?"

"Gone," said Boone.

"You lost it?"

"Yeah! I lost it!" he snapped.

"You went to that bar, didn't you? Last night in Evanston. You said that money was *ours*, Boone. You said we were a team."

Boone raised his hand to strike again. Chess held up his arm as a fragile defense. It was the only defense he was allowed. Otherwise, the response would be far worse. Fortunately, the strike never came.

"I don't answer to you!" Boone declared. "I was tryin' to get more money for *both* of us. It just didn't work out."

Chess straightened up. "It's okay. We'll just find another park."

"Are you kidding?" said Boone. "Look at that sky! In a few hours this whole town'll be under a foot of snow. All the parks will be empty."

"What about my jacket?" Chess asked meekly. "You said on the next take I could buy a jacket and a new pair—"

"You're not paying attention," said Boone. "We barely got enough to reach Las Vegas as it is. In Vegas you ain't gonna need a jacket anyway."

"But you promised," Chess persisted. "You said no matter what—"

Boone exploded. "It ain't gonna happen! Get it through your thick skull! You want a jacket, Chess? You want shoes? You're just gonna have to get them the old fashioned way."

The old-fashioned way. Chess understood all too well. It was the same way he'd gotten nearly everything he owned over the last eighteen months. But Chess didn't like it. At a Kmart in Denver, the manager had almost nabbed him with some underwear and a chocolate Santa Claus. He'd had to drop the loot and run. What they'd done in the park today seemed a whole lot easier. And somehow, more noble.

"So you want a jacket and shoes, or what?" Boone asked again.

Chess lifted up his sneaker and pulled the sole away from the heel, exposing his ankle. "Yeah," he said morosely. "I guess I'd better."

"That's all you had to say."

Boone turned right on 9th South, looking for a store. It would be a quick detour, then they'd be on the road again. Bound for Las Vegas.

Las Vegas, thought Chess. City of lights, casinos, and dancing girls.

Dancing girls.

He turned to his uncle. "Could my mother have been in Vegas, Boone?"

"Your mother is dead," said Boone. "I've told you that a million—"

"I know, I know," Chess interrupted. "What I mean is, was she *good* enough . . . was she *pretty* enough that she coulda performed in Vegas?"

Boone replied in an exhausted tone, as if he'd already answered a hundred similar questions. "Sure, Chess. She was the best. She coulda performed anywhere she wanted. For all I know, she *did* perform in Las Vegas. Back then, she was bouncin' around this country like a pinball."

Chess nodded to himself. He might have guessed

as much. Whatever his mother had done, he knew that she could only have been the best.

He felt tempted to reach into his pocket and retrieve the photograph. It was the only picture he owned of his mother. Actually, it was three pictures, connected together. He and his mother were sitting inside one of those photo booths at a carnival or shopping mall. The event had slipped his memory, but he'd been told the date was June 13th, his fourth birthday. Only the middle one clearly showed his mother's face; the others were obscured by creases and bends. Chess thought she looked beautiful, but she also looked weary, full of loneliness—a condition to which he could easily relate. He decided not to take the pictures out of his pocket. Boone would only taunt him, and he was not in the mood to be taunted.

Boone turned right again on 13th East. After a few blocks they found a plaza with a Shopko, a Payless shoe store, and a dozen other shops. Chess would have himself a new jacket and sneakers in no time.

Three

❦

MY TURN, THOUGHT Artemus. Now that all the morbid ceremonies surrounding his brother's memory were concluded, they might finally give *his* birthday their exclusive attention, starting with the customary hunt for expensive presents.

"What kind of things do you want this year?" asked Jordan Holiday as he guided the Lexus east on I-80.

"I want to shop for my own stuff," said Artemus from the backseat.

"You don't want any surprises?" asked his mother, Charlotte.

"Nah," said Artemus. "Just give me the Visa."

"Where would you like to go?" asked Jordan. "J & J Hobby? Toys 'R' Us?"

"Nordstrom," said Artemus.

His father made a wry expression. "Nordstrom? You want *clothes* for your birthday? When I was your age, the last thing I wanted was—"

"I want to go to the one at Fashion Place Mall."

"Artie, that's clear on the other side of town," Jordan protested.

"There's a Nordstrom right off 13th East," his sister, Amber, informed them. "In the Sugarhouse Center."

"That's a Nordstrom *Rack*," said Artemus with acute distaste. "It's clearance stuff and returns. Barely better than D.I."

Jordan bristled. Thirty years ago, growing up in South Salt Lake, his family would have considered a trip to the Deseret Industries thrift store the highlight of the month. He feared that his son was becoming precisely the kind of snob he used to loathe as a kid. Then again, he and his wife could only blame themselves. Artemus already owned nearly every toy known to humankind—enough for *two* children. Maybe that was the problem. He and Charlotte were still shopping for twins.

Jordan put his foot down. "Nordstrom Rack will have to do."

"But Dad," moaned Artemus, "that stuff is ancient history. I want to go to Fashion Place."

"It *is* his birthday," reminded Charlotte.

Jordan blew out a frustrated sigh. Birthday or no

birthday, it was time to submit to reason. "Artie," he said, "I just can't see making a forty-five minute detour when the Sugarhouse Center is just off the next exit. It's getting late, and we're all tired—"

"You wouldn't be so tired if we'd shopped first and *then* went to the cemetery," said Artemus.

Jordan became exasperated. "All right! We'll go to Fashion Place! I'll turn around at the next exit."

Artemus surveyed the irritated expressions all around. "Just forget it. I don't want to go shopping. Great birthday, as usual."

"Don't be that way," pleaded his mother. "You know this day is . . . difficult . . ."

"Once in a while, I wish it would be just *my* birthday," said Artemus.

"We're going to the Sugarhouse Center," said his father firmly. "And we *will* go shopping for birthday presents. Understand?"

Artemus was silent.

Jordan's shoulders drooped. Maybe his son had a point. It was a hard time of year for everyone. Tears sprang from his wife's eyes without cause. Concentration was difficult. He often had to take long walks to clear his head. It might have been a little better if Andrew had lost his life in some other way—natural causes, or an obvious act of God. But it was the *way* his son had died that left his heart an open wound. So his surviving son had never really known a pleasant, stress-free birthday. Not since the age of three.

"I'll make you a promise," said Jordan. "If you don't find anything you like, we'll hop right back in the car and drive over to Fashion Place. Okay?"

"Fine," said Artemus, his resentment still festering. He glanced at his sister. Amber was rolling her eyes. He made a rude face back at her. She was the zombie queen. They were *all* zombies.

As they pulled into the Sugarhouse Center, Charlotte declared, "A birthday isn't a birthday without surprises. Your father and I will visit some of the other stores while you shop for clothes. Amber, you go with your brother."

She shrank in her seat and muttered, "Great."

The Sugarhouse Center bustled with holiday shoppers. Snow had started falling heavily. Before finding a parking place, Jordan and Charlotte dropped off the children in front of Nordstrom Rack. The plan was to meet at the Olive Garden restaurant for a special birthday dinner in an hour.

Jordan handed over his Visa Gold and told Artemus his limit was a hundred dollars.

"Yeah, yeah," said Artemus. He headed toward the entrance, Amber trailing. When they got inside, he said to his sister, "You don't have to stay with me."

"I didn't plan to," she retorted, and off she went toward the girls' section.

* * *

Boone Folsom whipped into the parking space as soon as the other car pulled out, entirely ignoring the man and woman in the black Lexus who had been patiently waiting with their turn signal blinking.

"You snooze, you lose." He laughed.

The man in the Lexus gave him an irritated look and drove on. If the situation had been reversed, Boone would have left a nice long key scratch from one end of the Lexus to the other. He wasn't worried about a similar retaliation. His Buick already looked like it had been through three world wars. Further vandalism might only *improve* its appearance.

Boone shifted the car into park and said to Chess, "You go ahead."

"You ain't comin' with me, Boone?"

"I was up 'til three in the morning, Chess. I'm just gonna listen to some tunes and catch some Zs."

Chess became nervous. "Who's gonna distract the clerks?"

"It's a clothing store," said Boone impatiently. "All you gotta do is slip the new clothes on in the dressing room and walk out. You ain't gonna have no trouble."

"What if they see me?"

"You can run, can't ya?"

"What if they chase me?"

22

"Chess, don't you got a brain in your head?" He sat up and surveyed the plaza. "There." He pointed toward an office building at the northeast corner with a three-story parking garage. "You get into trouble, run in there. They'll never find you."

"But Boone—"

"I'm tired!" he hollered. "We got a whole night of drivin' ahead of us. Just get it done. And hurry! If you're not back here soon enough, I'll go on without you."

"You wouldn't do that."

"Wouldn't I? Don't test me. Now get outta the car."

Chess climbed out slowly. He'd always secretly feared that Boone would drive off and leave him one day. Then he truly *would* be an orphan. He'd tolerate every ounce of abuse and mistreatment his uncle could dish out, if it meant he could avoid that bitter distinction.

"Remember, Boone," said Chess. "We're a team, like you always say."

Boone settled back, closed his eyes, and said, "Just hurry up. I ain't goin' nowhere, Chess. And close the door. You're lettin' snow in here."

Chess closed the door. He turned away from the car and scanned all the various shops in the plaza. The one that caught his eye was called Nordstrom Rack. He crossed the parking lot and entered the store through the swinging glass doors. His eyes

23

were treated to a panorama of neatly dressed patrons, burgeoning rows of clothing, bright colors and smells. This was like a foreign world to Chess Folsom—just a place to visit now and then. A place to take advantage of. Christmas decorations were looped from wall to wall, which only made the place seem more alien. He'd never cared for Christmas. Unless, of course, he was watching reruns of *The Waltons* or *It's a Wonderful Life*. But in real life, things just weren't like that. Christmas was social workers passing out chintzy presents, usually marked with a tag that read simply, "for a boy." It also meant that stores were crammed with ten times more people than at other times during the year. Ten times more pairs of eyes. Taking the things he needed might prove to be a far more difficult prospect than usual.

Chess mulled around the store until he located the shoe aisle. There were *hundreds* of them; surely they wouldn't miss a single pair. The last time he'd gotten shoes, his foot size had been a six. He doubted if a six would fit anymore. He tried on some high-top sneakers, size seven. Just right. But after admiring them on his feet for another moment, he took them off. Just too white. Too clean. They contrasted too sharply with his other clothes. He'd never get out the door.

As he selected a second pair, more brown and

nondescript, a woman walked past the aisle, shot him a glance, and walked back again. Chess became nervous. He slipped the shoes into a box and went to find a more secluded place to put them on. Toward the back of the store he located the rack with winter jackets, but this spot was even more exposed than the shoe aisle. Nevertheless, he took a moment to check out the merchandise.

Every coat looked way too expensive. How could he possibly get out of the store with one of these? Maybe as he passed the cash register, he could make a break for it. Nah. Too risky. If they caught him, he'd be on a plane back to Florida fast as lightning. Back to another foster family. That was unthinkable. There had to be a better way.

He wandered along the back wall toward a rack with shirts and pants. Just ahead was a three-way mirror. In front of it stood a boy, partially hidden by the mirror's first panel.

"Stupid," Chess heard the boy declare, obviously displeased with the shirt he held up to his chest. The boy tossed the shirt back onto the rack without re-hanging it. He held up another shirt and pronounced the same verdict: "Stupid."

A strange feeling urged Chess to draw closer. The boy's face remained hidden. Only the back of his head was visible. He continued forward, and the boy's face fell into view. . . .

25

* * *

Too gaudy, thought Artemus as he inspected the shirt. He turned to see what it might look like in the side mirror. Then he turned to the next mirror—

The next mirror?

There *was* no "next" mirror. And yet a face was staring back at him. His *own* face! Artemus stood there, transfixed. The pair of eyes gaping back were also wide-open and frozen.

The two boys sized each other up for several seconds. The resemblance was remarkable. Even eerie. They both had the same small, upturned nose. The same slightly protruding ears. The same cloudy blue eyes. The same thin, blond hair. There were differences. One had fuller, rounder cheeks, while the other looked more gaunt. More hard. One had a freckle on his neck while the other had a small scar under his chin. But unless someone was *straining* to find distinguishing characteristics, the similarity was uncanny.

And yet for Artemus Holiday and Chess Folsom, such similarities quickly faded. It took only an instant for them to focus on the far more obvious and pressing *differences*—differences in clothing, grooming, demeanor, even odor!—each of which offended the other boy for opposite reasons. They were from diametrically opposed universes. It became obvious as they glared into each other's eyes

26

that neither saw any two things the same way. Nothing was shared—no two opinions, no two perspectives, no two *anything*. This entire transfer of emotion, intelligence, and instinct occurred in a matter of four or five seconds.

"You got a problem?" asked Artemus curtly.

"No, I don't got a problem," Chess replied just as curtly.

"Then why are you staring at me, squidhead?"

Artemus turned back to the mirror. Chess remained a second longer, searching for a comeback remark. When nothing came to him, he took satisfaction in hesitating as long as possible.

Artemus looked at Chess again. "You still here?"

Chess finally moved on, strutting as best he could to maintain some semblance of cool.

Artemus laughed inside. *What an idiot! They'll let* anybody *in this place.*

Chess made his way toward the front of the store. Resentment coiled in his guts, although he wasn't sure why. The boy hadn't said anything all that much ruder than any other kid. Usually in such situations Chess could deliver a crushing comeback, but his mind had drawn a blank.

Forget about it, he told himself. He just wanted to get out of there. The shoes were enough. Boone was right. In Las Vegas he wouldn't need a jacket. He just needed to find a place to slip on the shoes. Then he'd be gone.

As he neared the front of the store, he surveyed his escape route. He watched a lady loaded down with purchases try to exit through the front door. She set off some sort of alarm.

"Sorry," said the cashier. "I forgot to remove one of the thingamajigs."

As the alarm was silenced, Chess became terrified. *An alarm?* He'd never stolen from a ritzy place that tagged their merchandise with sensors that set off alarms. Did they tag *everything*? Was there a hidden sensor somewhere on his shoes? He detoured into a side aisle and opened the box. He couldn't find any evidence of a "thingamajig." What if it was imbedded inside the heel?

He looked back toward the door. He realized that he'd have to make a break for it. Someone might chase him. But he could still hide in the parking garage, like Boone had said.

He looked over his shoulder to see if the coast was clear. The opening at the end of the aisle framed the boy who had been so rude. The little snob was moving away with several pairs of pants over his arm, apparently headed toward the dressing rooms.

Chess let a grin climb his cheeks. An idea was born. A mischievous and marvelous idea.

* * *

Pretty slim pickin's, Artemus thought. But he *did* like the pants he'd selected. Both pairs. He'd just have to hope they fit.

He passed the layaway counter and entered the dressing room. The stalls were lined up along the right wall with about a foot of space at the bottom, like a public rest room. He glanced underneath to see which ones were free, and entered the second stall from the end. He hung up his coat, then slipped off his shoes and pants and laid them on the bench. The first trousers he tried on were a bit "high water." He must have grown some since the last time he'd been shopping.

As he tried on the second pair, he was vaguely aware that someone had entered the stall beside him. He thought nothing of it. The second pair was also high water. He grumbled to himself and exited the stall without putting on his old clothes, determined to return shortly with two more pairs that were slightly longer.

As soon as Artemus was gone, a pair of quick hands reached underneath the stall and snatched his shoes and pants from the bench.

It only took Artemus a few minutes to find two more trousers the right length. Heading back toward the dressing room, he noticed out of the corner of his eye the vagrant boy he'd confronted a few minutes earlier. The boy emerged from the dressing

29

rooms and made a beeline down the hat aisle to the other side of the store. Artemus only caught a glimpse of him through the tall clothing racks.

Strange, thought Artemus. He didn't remember the boy wearing a coat before. Now he was sporting a dark suede jacket that looked very similar to . . .

Artemus stiffened. He peered through the clothing racks, desperate to catch another glimpse. The boy was walking very fast toward the exit.

It couldn't be, thought Artemus. *He wouldn't dare try to steal—*

Artemus dashed into the dressing room and threw open the stall. His clothes were gone! Not only his coat, but his *pants and shoes*! The neighboring stall was also sitting open. On the bench sat the tattered clothing he'd seen the boy wearing earlier.

Artemus rushed out of the dressing room. "I've been robbed!" he shouted, thinking somehow this might inspire decent citizens everywhere to take action. Instead, the shoppers gaped at him, as if *he* were the criminal.

Artemus charged full throttle toward the store entrance. He remained shoeless, and without a coat. Around his waist still hung the unpurchased pair of high-water pants. He rushed past the register and burst out onto the sidewalk. It was almost dark; a half inch of snow had fallen. Finding the thief seemed hopeless. Nevertheless, his eyes looked in the direction indicated by a single pair of tracks, and—*there he was!* The vagrant boy! Still wearing his coat, pants, and shoes as he made a speedy flight eastward across the parking lot.

"Stop, thief!" Artemus cried.

Chess spun around briefly, then picked up steam as he ran toward the parking garage.

Artemus stood there in his socks, teeth grinding. He wasn't going to let the kid get away with this. Nobody took advantage of Artie Holiday. Especially a no-account hoodlum.

Amber emerged from the store. "Artie, what are you doing?"

He had no time to answer questions. He was sure he could still catch the thief. After all, he'd had the fastest time for the fifty-yard dash in the whole fifth grade. So despite the snow, despite his lack of shoes, he bolted across the pavement.

"Artie!" his sister cried. The store manager came outside as well, but nobody joined Artemus in the chase.

Chess glanced back again. *Uh-oh.* The kid was coming after him. In socks, no less! *He must have really liked this coat.* Chess kicked his legs even faster. He'd almost reached the parking garage. Inside, he hoped to find a secluded corner and wait it out. It shouldn't take long. How far could his pursuer keep up the chase without shoes?

As he entered the garage, he glanced back. The lunatic was still chasing him. He'd actually cinched the gap quite a bit.

"Give me back my clothes, you thief!" Artemus yelled.

Chess was impressed that this kid could run so fast in sopping socks. He turned again, darting past the rows of cars and up the cement incline to the second level, panting hard. He needed to find a place to hide and rest. The boy's echoes of "Stop, thief!" were drawing closer. Chess continued around the inclining driveway toward the third level.

As he rounded another corner, he pressed his back to the wall, fighting for breath. His pursuer no longer shouted. Surely he was equally winded. Maybe he'd given up.

Then Chess heard panting. He went a little farther and ducked behind a Mercury Tracer, crouching low enough to see underneath the car. After a few seconds, Artemus's feet appeared. He was walking now, seemingly confident that his prey was trapped. Chess saw that one of his wet socks was missing. Artemus stumbled once as he stepped on a sharp pebble. After a limp or two, he pressed on, pausing to look between each vehicle. Chess wondered if he could take him. A snotty brat like him was probably as soft as a marshmallow. One good punch and it would be over. Still, if he could avoid getting blood on his new clothes, he would.

At last, Artemus did the smart thing and got down on his hands and knees. As he scanned beneath the vehicles, he soon met the eyes of his prey. "Gotcha!" he shouted.

Chess blasted out from between the cars. Artemus gritted his teeth and lunged after him. The two boys scrambled across a section of ramp that was exposed to the weather, carpeted by slippery snow. Artemus leaned forward. He'd almost reached him. As Chess careened around the next corner to the uppermost parking level, Artemus pounced. But as he grabbed the back of Chess's collar, a pair of blazing headlights came barreling down from the upper level. Chess had doubled up his fist, ready to deliver the all-critical punch. He watched Artemus's eyebrows rise in horror. He spun. It was too late. Both boys shrieked.

The driver of the Nissan pickup slammed on his brakes, but the snow impeded his ability to stop. In desperation, Artemus twisted sideways. Chess froze in his tracks. He shielded his face, closed his eyes, and awaited disaster.

Artemus felt the impact against his hip. He tumbled toward the containment barrier at the edge of the building. As Chess was hit, a flash of blinding whiteness exploded behind his eyes, followed by pain as his body folded up and over the hood of the vehicle. As the brakes finally screeched to a halt, Chess toppled off the hood.

Artemus felt another bruising impact as he hit the containment barrier. He grunted in agony, flipping over the other side and twisting into a spectacular fall—two and a half stories! In a blur of terror, he clutched at the limbs of the scrubby elms that overlooked the barrier. The brittle branches ripped through his hands. He was swallowed up by the darkness.

For both boys, the lights had gone out. Their last emotions were horror and confusion. But it was nothing compared to the horror and confusion that awaited them when they awakened.

Four

❧

THE DRIVER OF the Nissan pickup was drunk. His fear that he might have killed someone had at least given him the presence of mind to stagger back to his office, interrupt the Christmas party, and ask for help. Police and paramedics arrived ten minutes later. Jordan and Charlotte Holiday arrived as well, led by Amber, who'd watched her brother enter the parking garage.

When Chess creaked open his eyes, paramedics were hovering all around, attaching instruments to his arms and chest and strapping him into a back brace. Flashing lights washed over the walls of the garage. He felt groggy and disoriented. He couldn't see very well. His face had smashed against the

Nissan's hood. His eyes were swollen, and he could taste blood.

Another face hovered above him, someone he didn't recognize—a lady with one of those fancy hairdos. She was holding his hand. "He's awake," she announced to two people behind her—a man about forty wearing a sports jacket, and a girl with braces.

The lady squeezed his hand. "I'm here, Artie."

Artie? thought Chess, wrinkling his brow. *Who the heck is Artie?*

The man knelt beside him. "Can you see all right? Do you recognize us?"

Chess shook his head. The woman stroked his hair and fought back tears. "It's all right," she told him. "I'm not going to leave you."

The paramedics carried the stretcher toward the ambulance. Chess caught a snatch of the conversation as the police interrogated the handcuffed driver of the pickup.

"There was another one," the driver told the cops, his voice slurred.

"Another what?" asked the officer.

"Kid. I hit two. Two kids."

"Uh-huh," said the officer skeptically. "How many fingers am I holding up?" He held up two.

"Four?" the man replied.

"That's what I thought." The officer helped the drunk man into the back of the patrol car.

Chess was hoisted into the ambulance. The woman with the fancy hairdo climbed in after him. The man in the sports jacket touched his arm reassuringly and informed the woman, "We'll follow you to St. Mark's."

They shut the ambulance doors. The strange lady continued to grip his hand. *Who are these weirdos?* thought Chess. *Why is this person fawning all over me?* Then he guessed it. She must have been a passenger in the pickup. She was the drunk man's wife, and she felt guilty. But then who were the guy in the sports jacket and the girl in braces?

Finally, Chess found the strength to inquire, "Where's Boone?"

"Who's Boone, Artie?" asked the lady. "What's a *boone*?"

What was she *talking* about? Why did she keep calling him Artie?

"What's wrong with him?" the woman asked the paramedic.

"He took quite a hit," the paramedic replied. "He may be delirious. Let's try to keep him alert."

Delirious? thought Chess. He may have felt like he'd just been socked by a 747, but he was definitely *not* delirious. He was perfectly clear. Because of this, a tide of panic was rising inside him. *Where was Boone?* Would he meet him at the hospital? No way.

37

Boone wouldn't go within a mile of anyone in uniform. No doctors. No police.

He's gone, thought Chess. His worst fears had finally been realized. He knew that he'd never see his uncle again.

Once again, Chess was alone in the world.

Well, it's over, thought Boone, standing outside in the falling snow, watching the police lights color the walls of the parking garage above him. *It was a good racket while it lasted. But all good things must inevitably come to an end.*

He was surprised when he saw the ambulance arrive. Had someone been hurt? Was it Chess? Stupid question. Of *course* it was Chess. Was he dead? Boone had no way of knowing, and he wasn't about to go up there and find out.

He watched, cursing, as the ambulance sped away. How could Chess have managed to get himself hurt? The kid was a born klutz. Shame. All those months of meticulous training, wasted.

Boone felt the pocket of his Levi's jacket. He still had about five hundred dollars—money he'd carefully hidden from Chess. The plan was still to reach Las Vegas. He'd developed a system for beating poker slots that he was sure would quickly double his money. He could then triple and quadruple it.

Maybe it was better this way, thought Boone. In

Vegas, he'd have had no place to stow Chess. Now he could—

Boone did a double take. There was movement in the snow-covered bank of trees and shrubbery to the left of where he stood, just below the ledge where all the commotion was happening.

He approached the bushes. It was dark, and he had no flashlight. Nevertheless, he perceived what appeared to be a person tangled up in the brambles, unconscious and half-frozen.

"Chess?" Boone asked. "That you, kid?"

The boy could only groan in reply.

Boone reached in through the branches and latched on to the boy's torso. He dragged him out, cussing for all the scratches he incurred on his knuckles. He carried the boy into the light and brushed the snow off his face. Yup, it was Chess all right. He looked a mess. There was a nice goose egg on the side of his head. Somehow he'd lost his shoes and one sock. But at least he'd managed to steal some new clothes. The pants even had the tags still attached.

The boy stirred a little, but otherwise made no effort to regain consciousness. Boone wondered if he might need a doctor. If he'd fallen from the ledge, there could easily be broken bones. No way to tell until he woke up. Boone decided he'd better get back on the road. If Chess got any worse, or if he woke up whining about a broken limb, he might consider dropping him off outside some emergency room, then making himself scarce. He didn't like the idea. If the authorities identified Chess, they'd know Boone was in the area. Maybe it would be better if he just let the boy . . .

No reason to think about that now. Surely the kid would be fine. The partnership between them remained in force. At least, for the moment.

Five

❦

THIS LADY IS *beginning to bug me*, thought Chess.

It wasn't the fact that she was fawning all over him, making sure the doctors and nurses gave him the proper attention. He sort of liked that. It had been a long time since a nice lady—a *genuinely* nice lady—had given him any attention at all. What bugged him—what *floored* him, as a matter of fact— was that she was actually suffering under the delusion that he was her *son*.

At first he ignored it. He was in enough shock as it was; let the crazy lady think whatever she wanted. But now that he'd reached the hospital, now that his thoughts were perfectly sharp, he was sorely tempted to grab her by the collar and yell, "Look! My

41

name is *not* Artie! Got it? It's Chess! Now, let's say it together. *Chess!*"

He didn't say it. Why did he hesitate? Out of fear, he supposed. No telling what a crazy person might do if you disagreed with them. And yet he couldn't quite convince himself that she was crazy. Maybe she had a good reason for pretending he was her son. Maybe it was some kind of scam. But that didn't feel right either. Her actions were too sincere. She *really* and *truly* believed he was a kid named Artie!

Chess wanted to see his face in a mirror. That blow must have turned it into meatloaf. How else could you explain such a bizarre case of mistaken identity? His mug must have been so messed up, he'd pass for *anyone*!

He realized there was a mirror right across from his bed, so he looked at his reflection as the doctors examined him for broken bones. His face did have some swelling. He had a black eye—maybe *two* black eyes. His nose was beet red, and there was a dark bruise on his cheekbone. Otherwise, he looked the same as he'd always looked.

His imagination sifted through other explanations. What if he'd passed into a parallel universe? What if his name really *was* Artie, and this really *was* his mother? Or what if aliens had taken over the bodies of every man, woman, and child on earth?

This ruse of pretending his name was Artie was merely part of a devious plot to control his mind. Such options might have seemed far-fetched, but no more far-fetched than the final option: *Chess Folsom looked exactly like this lady's son!*

But if that was true, where was her *real* son? How long could this charade go on before the *real* Artie waltzed through the door? And by the way, who *was* her real son? Surely not the kid who'd been chasing him. That jerk didn't look anything like him.

The lady continued to hold his hand while the doctor pressed a butterfly bandage to the cut on his cheek. "You're doing great, Artie," she said. "Dad and Amber should be here any minute. This hasn't been the best birthday for you, has it?"

Chess shook his head. "No, ma'am. Can't say as it has."

This is too weird, thought Chess. He couldn't go on with this any longer. He decided to come clean as soon as the doctor finished with the cut.

Just then, the man and girl from the parking garage arrived. The man looked distraught. Both of them approached eagerly. The man touched his forehead.

"How ya doing, kiddo?" he asked.

Chess gawked back. *Oh, no. Another one.*

"The doctor says nothing is broken," the lady reported.

The man turned to the doctor in disbelief. "Nothing?"

"As far as I can determine, he didn't suffer anything worse than a few scrapes and bruises," said the doctor. "And of course a nice pair of shiners. He's very lucky."

The man melted with gratitude. He put his arm around the woman and said tearfully, "Thank God."

Next, the girl approached. "How ya feelin', little brother? I see you got your clothes back. How far did you have to chase that thief before he dropped your shoes and pants?"

They do *think I'm that kid!* Chess marveled. But that was absurd! He and that kid were as different as night and day. Only an idiot could ever believe . . . !

Chess recalled his first impression when he'd laid eyes on that boy at the mirror. *Okay,* he confessed to himself. Maybe they did look a *little* similar. But similar enough to fool the kid's own parents? Maybe it was the bruises. As soon as they started to heal, the mistake would be obvious. But by then Chess would be long gone. Even now, he looked around for a way to give everyone the slip.

"Artie," said the man, "there's a policeman outside."

Chess's heart froze. "A p-p-policeman?" He could see the cop out in the entrance area. He was walking toward them!

"I thought you might like to tell him about the boy

who stole your clothes," the man continued. "You know, give a description. Maybe they can catch him. The police can inform his parents. That way he won't cause any more accidents."

"You mean he's missing?" asked Chess.

"I'm afraid he got away," said the officer. He took out a pad of paper. "Do you think you could describe what he looks like? Distinguishing characteristics? Anything at all?"

Chess shook his head. "No, sir. It was dark. I didn't see him too well. But I know he was a lot older. In fact, I think he had a beard."

The policeman raised an eyebrow. "He was older, and he could still fit into your clothes?"

Chess thought about this. "I think he was a midget. Yeah, he was real small. Like one a them guys who rides racehorses."

The officer wrote it down. "Midget, eh? Possible racehorse jockey."

"That's right," said Chess. "With a beard. That's all I saw."

The woman scrutinized Chess. "Are you being honest, Artie? This is a policeman—"

"*Sure* I'm bein' honest."

"What's with the Southern drawl?" asked the man.

"Nothin'," said Chess.

The policeman put away his notepad. "Well, he's had quite an ordeal. I won't bother you any more with this tonight. Get the boy home and get some rest. Maybe he'll remember more tomorrow. Give us a call."

Chess watched him leave and breathed a sigh of relief. His freedom was assured for at least one more day.

"Can he go?" the man asked the doctor.

"Yes," the doctor replied. "Watch him closely for the next several hours. If there's any dizziness or vomiting, let us know immediately."

The man squeezed Chess's arm. "Did you hear that? We can take you home! Everything's gonna be okay."

Chess was incredulous. No way was he going home with these freaks! He'd figured it out. They ran a torture chamber. This was a scheme to collect more victims.

"Let's go home," the woman told Chess. "Maybe we can still salvage part of your birthday. Would you like that? Your present is in the car."

Chess raised an eyebrow. "Did you say . . . present?"

"You still haven't opened my present either," said the girl. "It's at home."

Chess tried to sound nonchalant. "Just how many . . . presents are we talkin' about? Are there even more?"

The lady and the girl laughed.

The man mussed up his hair. "I can tell you're feeling better already."

Six

❧

ONE MOMENT SUSPENDED in time.

The memory was like an iron brand, searing hot and stabbing down, never fading or healing, blistering forever the minds of Jordan Holiday and his son, Artemus. The image was always there, lurking in the wings, waiting patiently for its cue to take center stage. Usually it came at night, as they fought for sleep.

For young Artemus, the memory comprised sound as much as image. It was his brother's cry for help, a cry for his father. Artemus had been told to run home and tell his mother to call 911. He knew Andrew was in trouble. Serious trouble. So little Artemus, all of three years old, raced up the icy slope to faithfully fulfill his father's request, never faltering or turning back. He heard only the cries, the piercing, desperate cries that shattered the sky. Then suddenly, the cries of his brother ended. There was silence. Artemus stopped. The wails of his father filled the void.

Little Artemus had to see. He turned back. •

The ancient memory of what he saw on that awful Christmas morning haunted him even now, *especially* now, as he slumped in the seat of a stranger's car, engulfed by a terrible headache, careening across the snowswept hills of southern Utah, traveling south along Interstate 15. Artemus stirred, trying to flee from the image. He groaned, trying to snuff it out. But he couldn't escape it. Nor could he regain consciousness. And because he was helpless, the image was relentless.

The image was no less relentless for his father, presently hundreds of miles away in Salt Lake. He, too, tossed and turned in the night. In his dreams he put forth his arm, reaching across the blinding-white expanse to where the cries of his son reverberated. Just another yard. Another inch. Suddenly the little hand slipped away. *It slipped away!*

"Andyyyyy!"

Jordan awakened in his wife's arms, trembling. His pillow was soaked in sweat and tears.

"It's all right," Charlotte consoled, rocking him gently. "It's all right now."

He wept into her shoulder for a minute longer. He could feel Charlotte weeping too. This had been a regular, silent ritual between them for many nights over the last eight years.

Jordan might have thought that after eight years, his grief would subside and the image would finally fade. Instead, it had sharpened and amplified; in fact, the pain had sunk so deep now that he could no longer reach it. What frightened him more was that no one else could help him reach it either. Not anymore. Not his wife. Not his children. Not even his God. What would become of a man who could no longer find sanctuary from his torment?

Finally, Jordan drew a deep breath and sat up straight. His wife sent him a painful smile.

"I guess it was the accident tonight," he said. "It must have . . . stirred up things. I don't know what I'd do if I . . . lost both—" He paused and swallowed.

"I know," said Charlotte.

Jordan started to rise. "I better check on him."

Charlotte stopped him. "It's all right. I already have. He's sleeping soundly."

Jordan lay back down.

Charlotte added, "I might take him back in tomorrow."

"To the doctor?" he asked.

"Do *you* think he's acting normal?"

"Well," said Jordan, "he certainly acted impressed by his birthday presents—for a change. If you think *that's* abnormal—"

"Jordan, he couldn't remember where his bedroom was."

"He was just confused."

"What about the way he's talking?"

"What about it? All last month he spoke with a British, Cockney—whatever that accent was."

"But that was to practice. You'd think the school was doing *Gone With the Wind* instead of *A Christmas Carol*."

"He'll be okay," said Jordan. "Tomorrow, everything will be business as usual."

This didn't console her. "Business as usual" was never all too "usual" at this time of year.

Charlotte sighed. "Am I making too much of it?"

Jordan considered his answer carefully. "No. You're allowed."

The words left an ominous ring. She *was* allowed. Few mothers on this earth had earned more right to be overprotective. The conversation stopped. Charlotte and Jordan attempted to fall asleep again. The clock read almost 3:00 A.M. before either of them succeeded.

Once again, the blinding-white expanse seared Jordan's vision. The cries of his little son reverberated on the night wind.

Seven

IS IT OVER? Chess wondered.

Had the dream come to an end? He roused from slumber and looked up at the ceiling fan overhead. His eyes scanned the bedroom walls, decorated with posters of luxury sports cars, exotic tropical beaches, and cinematic monsters. It was one of the largest bedrooms he'd ever slept in, with one of the largest beds—a four-posted oak monstrosity that must have weighed as much as a tank. Every toy in every television commercial he'd ever seen lined the shelves along all four walls. From the ceiling hung numerous models of remote-control airplanes, including the one they'd presented to him last night—a Lance Bandit biplane with a wingspan of nearly six feet.

What was he thinking? They hadn't purchased it for *him*. They'd purchased it for their *son*.

Reality check, thought Chess. He ran the events of the past twelve hours through his mind: *I'm in Salt Lake City, Utah. I'm living with a family of crazy people who think my name is Artie. Boone is gone, likely five hundred miles away by now.*

There was a full-length mirror on the bedroom door. He climbed out from under the covers and stood in front of it. The swelling on his face had gone down, but the bruises on his cheek and around his eyes had deepened in color. Twin black eyes. He looked totally stupid.

Chess looked around the room. *I gotta get outta here,* he decided. By now, the *real* Artie had surely shown up. As Chess reached for the doorknob, he half expected to find it locked. The police would already be downstairs waiting for him. In their hands would be a pair of handcuffs and an airline ticket to Florida.

He tried the door. To his surprise, it was *open*.

Simultaneously, a voice shattered the bedroom silence.

"Artie?"

Chess nearly leaped out of his skin. It was like a voice from heaven, pronouncing once and for all that his new name was indeed Artie, and he'd better get used to the idea.

54

The voice boomed again. "Artie, are you awake?"

He recognized it now. It was the voice of the lady with the hairdo—his "mother." He searched and found the intercom beside the light switch. Leaning in close, he stammered, "Uh, yes. Yes, ma'am."

"Enough with the 'ma'am' stuff, kiddo. How are you feeling? Are you hungry?"

"Yes, ma'—" He caught himself. "Yes, I am."

"Would you like to come down to breakfast?"

"S-sure. I'll, uh, be right down."

He suddenly felt conspicuous standing in a stranger's bedroom wearing nothing but a pair of Fruit of the Looms—the only remaining stitch of clothing that was legitimately his. He stepped over to the tall, cherry-wood dresser and diffidently opened each of the drawers.

Holy Moses! This guy had enough clothes to dress an orphanage. One drawer alone was set aside exclusively for socks. When he opened the closet, his eyes widened again. Make that enough clothes to dress a small South American country. Only *kings* had closets this big. Kings and movie stars.

Chess selected the least ostentatious wardrobe he could find—a pair of Wranglers with a yellow shirt. He opened the doorway to the rest of the house.

The room where he'd slept was situated on the second floor, overlooking a balcony above a living room and formal dining room. Wide, tinted windows comprised much of the opposite wall, bathing the room in subdued morning sunlight. He'd known it was a nice house last night when they'd pulled into the driveway, but only in daylight could he appreciate the full effect. Not that it was Buckingham Palace. As far as he could tell, there were no full-time servants or maids, and the yard was only modestly large. Neighbors were well within spitting distance.

Chess's first impulse was to scan the area for steely-eyed policemen or frumpy social workers, but there were no signs of an ambush. The only person in sight was the man—his so-called father—reading a newspaper.

Cripes! He didn't even know these people's names! Here he'd spent the night in their house, and he wasn't even sure who they were. What was he supposed to call them? Mom and Dad?

No way. He couldn't stomach it. He and Boone may have run every scam ever invented from one end of the country to the other, but he still couldn't bring himself to address two complete strangers as Mom and Dad. The titles were hallowed somehow. There were some lines that Chess wouldn't cross.

The man looked up. "*There* he is!" he announced.

The neighboring bedroom door opened, and the girl emerged. She took one look at him and teased, "Oh my gosh! It's Ricky Raccoon!"

Chess might have slugged her if she wasn't supposed to be his sister. Then again, maybe that gave him the *right* to slug her.

The lady came out from the kitchen area to see him, her hands filled with a steaming plate of waffles. "Oh my," she said, assessing his bruises. "Do you feel well enough to go to school?"

"School?" He shook his head. "No. Not *that* well."

"Mom, you're forgetting," said the sister. "He *has* to go to school. Today is dress rehearsal."

"Dress rehearsal?" Chess repeated, as if he'd never heard the phrase before, which, in fact, he hadn't. He imagined a scene with everybody in school—boys included—wearing dresses and walking down a catwalk. This was Utah, right? He'd heard they did strange things in Utah.

"Oh, that's right," the mother recalled. "The play is tomorrow. Mrs. Svetson would kill you."

"You think they'll still let him perform?" asked the sister.

"Why not?" said the father. "He's supposed to be a street kid. They'll probably think black eyes are right in character. He only has six lines, anyway."

"The question is, does he feel up to it?" said the mother.

Chess shook his head again, this time vigorously. If these people thought he was gonna perform in a *play*, they had another thing coming. Not Chess

Folsom. Nooo way. He'd rather wear the dress. Once again, he felt the urge to flee.

"What exactly *is* wrong, Artie?" asked the father. "Do you feel dizzy?"

"Yeah, dizzy."

"Headaches?"

"That too."

"Nausea?"

"Yes, sir."

"Stiffness in the joints?"

"Uh-huh."

"Hardening of the arteries?"

"Yeah."

The father smiled.

The sister laughed and made her way down the stairs. "Give me a break. He's just petrified that everybody's gonna call him Ricky Raccoon."

"If he wants to stay home, he can stay," said the mother. "He's been through enough. Rehearsal doesn't start until four. I can take him then. Come down to breakfast, honey."

Chess began to descend the stairs. All along the stairway hung family portraits and photographs. He paused to look at one where everybody wore matching T-shirts, like a baseball team. The resemblance between himself and the kid waving a baseball cap was undeniable. It was freaky. This whole *thing* was freaky. That kid in the picture might as well *be him*!

The longer he stared at the photo, the more his imagination took flight. Maybe it *was* him! Why *shouldn't* it be him? What made that kid any better than he was?

"One waffle or two?" the mother called up the stairs.

"Uh, two," said Chess. He continued to the bottom of the stairway, ignoring a picture of twin boys, toddlers, holding Easter baskets.

"If you're gonna let Artie miss school because of two black eyes," said the sister, pouring syrup, "I think I should miss school every time I get a big zit."

"The next time you get hit by a truck," said the mother, "you can stay home too."

Chess passed by a small end table with a three-foot artificial Christmas tree. Around it hung a dozen or so gold-colored bulbs that almost appeared as if they'd come already attached. Such was the extent of the family's seasonal adornments. Chess found this lack of holiday frills somewhat baffling—not at all how he imagined families should behave. Totally un-Walton-like.

But they made up for it as Chess tried to scarf down his first bite of waffle.

"Artie. The blessing," said the mother.

He stopped in mid-chew, awkwardly crossing his

arms over his chest like everyone else. He peeked several times as the man thanked his Heavenly Father for all of their food, asking that it might bless and nourish everyone present. The smell of hot, buttery waffles was driving him crazy. As soon as the prayer ended, he packed in another bite. He couldn't remember the last time he'd eaten a home-cooked breakfast. This alone made this bizarre ordeal well worth it. As he glanced up at all the faces around him, smiling and chewing, something even more peculiar struck him. He'd never in his life eaten a meal with folks who'd actually considered him a genuine, certified, real-life member of the family—whether it was all a big mistake or not. It was a weird feeling. Sorta nice.

On second thought, it wasn't nice at all. It was *sickening*. Sickening because it was a lie. As Chess took another bite, his eyes landed on those of the mother. She watched him with more intensity than the others. He looked down at his waffles, spreading the syrup into all of the little indentations. *She knows,* he thought. What an idiot to think he could fool the kid's own mother for very long.

And yet as he glanced back, the look in her eyes did not seem so much suspicious or accusing as . . . wistful.

Maybe I will *go to school,* thought Chess. But only because it might give him an opportunity to make a clean getaway. It was time. He couldn't stay in this place any longer. As soon as he could manage it, he was outta here.

That is, right after breakfast.

Eight

❧

SO *TIRED.*

Every effort he exerted to try and wake up was futile. Even in his dreams, he could feel people trying to rouse him. He could hear voices in his mind. The most persistent voice belonged to his father: *"Artie, time to wake up. Time for school, son. Don't argue with me. You're going to school. Do you hear me? Now get up!"*

And then his mother: *"Artie, you've slept long enough. Do you think you can sleep forever? Come on now. Please wake up."*

And even his sister: *"Hey, bonehead. Get up. All right. I'm taking all your hobby planes. And your Goosebumps collection. And your Game Boy. I mean it, Artie. Are you going to get up?"*

Even the threat of losing his most sacred posses-
sions couldn't rouse him. He just couldn't open his
eyes. In one dream he even saw Candee Reynolds,
the most beautiful girl in the fifth grade, leaning over
him with puckered lips, as if to awaken him from an
evil spell. But her kiss never quite landed. Those
lips just hovered there, waiting for him to sit up and
take them.

But he couldn't sit up. He couldn't move. Why
couldn't he *wake up*?

The most curious voice of all was one he didn't
recognize. He felt this person's hands lifting him.
Oddly, the voice didn't call him by name. It addressed him by an altogether different name. "How
ya doin', Chess?" it would ask. "You look good.
You're doin' great. Just sleep it off, kid."

The voice frightened him, even in his sleep. He
tensed whenever he heard it. It dredged up horrible
dreams. Once, after hearing it, a nightmare took hold
of his mind wherein he found himself surrounded by
water—*freezing* water, with sharp needles of ice
whirling around him. He was drowning. Gasping for
breath.

He'd become Andrew.

The last time he heard this voice was the most ter-
rifying of all. Perhaps because he was just beginning
to stir back to consciousness. "I'm going out, Chess,"

said the voice. "You'll be alone here for a while. Just take it easy." A door opened and shut.

Even in semiconsciousness, Artemus realized something was very wrong. He was not in the place where he should have been. Fear surged through his veins like acid. It was this fear that finally inspired him to raise his eyelids.

He was lying in a dark room. Slivers of light outlined a doorway. It was daytime. The curtains on the windows were unusually thick, as if designed to make someone think it was night.

He perceived a second bed to his right, then a bathroom. A light was on above the toilet. This allowed him to see the furnishings of the rest of the room. The wallpaper was covered with pink and yellow palm trees. There was a television bolted to the wall. Outside he could hear traffic and voices, car doors and laughter.

He tried to sit up. An excruciating headache was unleashed in his skull. He pressed his palm to his forehead and rolled out of bed. He felt a savage bruise on his hip and another one on his stomach. After staggering to the curtain, he pulled it back.

Outside was a parking lot, and beyond it a busy street. The sidewalks bustled with people. They were all dressed far more casually than he might have expected for wintertime; many wore T-shirts and shorts! Had he slept all winter? Was it July? Across the street stood a tall building with a massive marquee that read STARLIGHT HOTEL AND CASINO. Over his window loomed a weather-beaten neon sign flashing LAMP'USTER MOTE'—'AS VEGAS' FINEST, three Ls having burned out.

Las Vegas? thought Artemus. This didn't make any sense.

A phone. He had to call someone. He had to call home.

A phone sat on the night table. He stumbled toward it and raised the receiver. All at once, he forgot what he was doing. He stared at the phone, uncertain, as if staring at a strange new invention.

Ah yes, he remembered. *Call home. I have to call home.* But what was the number? He tried to concentrate. He couldn't recall his own phone number. A number he'd dialed a thousand . . .

Suddenly he felt as weak as a kitten. His head was swimming. All he wanted to do was close his eyes again. Go back to sleep. Everything would be normal when he awakened a second time. He'd be lying in his bedroom, staring up at his model airplanes.

Yes, that was the solution. It seemed so right. But right or not, it overcame him without choice.

Artemus didn't remember lying back on the bed. One second he was awake, and the next he was again a prisoner of his own dreams.

Nine

❦

"Now, Artemus, I want you to call me if you feel any sickness at all," said Charlotte Holiday.

Chess had learned his last name—that is, the last name of the family he was staying with—when he read it on the mailbox as they drove away from the house.

"Do you understand?" she continued.

Chess nodded and turned to walk away from the car. "Yeah, I understand." He turned back. "Uh, Mom?"

"Yes?"

Chess swallowed. He'd spoken the hallowed word. He'd called her *Mom*. Had he no shame whatsoever? As he recalled his question, he bit his tongue. He'd wanted a reminder of their phone number. What a dufus! She'd have become twice as suspicious as she already was.

Chess shook his head. "Never mind."

"I love you," she said.

Chess shuffled his feet. How was he supposed to respond to *that*? The sister in the backseat, whose name he still didn't know, saved him. "Come on, Mom," she clamored. "I'll be late!"

Charlotte said to Chess, "Remind Mr. Walruff to let you out ten minutes early for rehearsal. I'll be here at 3:15."

"Right," said Chess.

She put the car into gear. The sister looked at him through the window and curled her fingers around her eyes, reminding him that he still looked like a raccoon. Then she dropped her hands and smiled sympathetically. He smiled back. *She's not so bad,* he thought.

He surveyed the snow-covered school grounds. *Well, this is it,* he told himself. His best chance to escape. And yet he knew he couldn't go through with it. All during the ride to school, his resolve had steadily weakened. Besides, where was he supposed to go? Boone was history. He'd been abandoned in Salt Lake City, Utah. And yet, by the most peculiar of earthly phenomena, he'd acquired membership in an actual family. Surely it was temporary; such a miracle couldn't possibly be permanent. But only a cosmic numbskull would pass up such an opportunity while it stared him in the face.

The question remained: Where was the kid who'd chased him in the parking garage? Chess blocked this out. Who could say whether that kid were still in the same universe?

A boy approached Chess and said, "Wow, Artie, what happened to you?"

"I got hit by a truck," he replied.

"Really?" said the kid. "A truck did that to you?"

Chess smirked. "You should see the truck."

He made his way across the playground, where various lines were forming outside various doors. He attached himself to the kid who'd addressed him, hoping he might be in his same class and lead him to the appropriate line. The boy looked at him strangely as they neared the building.

"Where ya goin', Artie?"

"Uh, I don't know. Where *you* goin'?"

"Duh," said the kid. "Mr. Hunt's."

Chess tried the direct approach. "And where should I line up?"

"Disneyland," the kid said sarcastically. "Where do you think?"

"No, seriously. Where's the line for—" He tried to remember his teacher's name. *Man!* What was it? The lady had just said it. "—You know, my teacher."

"Are you makin' fun of me, Artie?"

"No, I—"

" 'Cause I hate it when people make fun of me. People are always makin' fun of me!"

"Forget it," said Chess. "Not important."

He walked away before the kid could spontaneously combust. There were dozens of lines all around the school. *This shouldn't be that hard,* he thought. Just find another line with kids close to his own age.

"Hi, Artie," crooned a voice from behind him.

Chess spun around to find himself face-to-face with an eleven-year-old goddess of beauty. She brushed a strand of auburn hair from her face as she winced. "Oooow. Did you get into a fight?"

Chess cocked his head. "Yeah, that's right."

"Who beat you up?"

His shoulders slumped. "Huh? Me? Are you kid—?"

She took him by the arm and led him toward one of the lines. "Boys can be so vicious. You're such a fast runner, Artie. Next time, you better just run. Don't you think?"

"Uh, I, uh—"

As they reached the line, more kids gathered to admire his wounds. Without exception, everyone called him Artemus or Artie. Somehow the voice of the masses made it official. He *was* Artemus Holiday. Why not accept it? What did he have to lose?

He overheard some of them saying his teacher's

name, which gave him confidence later that morning as the teacher's gaze centered squarely upon him.

"Mr. Holiday," the teacher said stuffily.

"Yes, Mr. Walrus?" asked Chess.

A gasp rippled through the room. With hoisted eyebrows, the teacher stood up from his chair, revealing a belly that hung well out over his desk. Chess swallowed hard as he realized that the name the other students had been using was not his actual name, nor was it complimentary.

"What did you say?" asked Mr. Walruff, glowering.

"Something really stupid?" he replied sheepishly.

Mr. Walruff scrutinized him, uncertain if it was just a slip. Eyes still thin, he said, "Please go before the class and identify the nation of India."

Chess nervously approached the unlabeled map of the world. He set the wooden pointer against the western United States.

"Congratulations," said the teacher. "You've just indicated South Dakota."

"Really?" said Chess. " 'Cause I been there. I know it has lotsa Indians."

The class laughed hysterically. Chess started to shrink again. Had he said something funny?

Mr. Walruff bit each word in half as he directed Chess, "Please—sit—down!"

After Chess returned to his seat, the auburn-haired

goddess behind him whispered, "I never knew you could be so cool, Artie."

"Cool" wasn't exactly the word Chess would have chosen, unless the first letter was replaced with an "f." In a single morning, he'd totally obliterated Artemus's standing to that of classroom cutup. But this was nothing compared to the change in Artie's reputation that he introduced at recess.

As a burly sixth grader tried to take cuts in front of him in the tetherball line, ordering him to "back off or I'll give you a fat lip to go with those black eyes," Chess promptly laid him out flat on the asphalt with a punch to the nose.

Unfortunately, this also landed him in the office of the principal, who in turn called Mrs. Holiday.

"Fighting?" Charlotte repeated into the phone. "That's impossible. My Artie never fights."

"Then how do you explain the two black eyes?" asked the principal.

After she told him about the accident, they concluded that Artemus must not be himself. It might be best if he took the afternoon off to be certain he'd fully recovered from his head injury.

Fifteen minutes later, Chess climbed into Charlotte's car. "What's going on?" she asked.

"Somebody had to do somethin' about that kid," said Chess. "He was bullying everyone on the playground."

Charlotte shook her head. "I don't understand it. This isn't like you. Ever since this accident, Artie, you've been . . ."

"Whatsa matter, Mom?" Chess teased. "You think aliens have taken over my brain?" He gave her a maniacal grin.

Charlotte looked at him. For a split second, the suggestion didn't seem all that outlandish. Then she smiled. "Just do me a favor. Talk normal for a while."

"What's normal?"

"Drop the Southern accent."

Chess grinned. "Would you rather I talked like I was from Utah?" He spoke in a thick western drawl. *"Well, howdy partner. I'm from Utah. Yuk, yuk, yuk."*

Charlotte laughed. To Chess, it was a wonderful sound. So fresh and real, as if she hadn't laughed for a very long time. She tried to readopt a grim, disciplinary tone. But it wasn't ten seconds before Chess had her laughing again.

She took him to lunch at Godfather's Pizza for the all-you-can-eat buffet—not exactly the punishment she'd envisioned during her drive to the school, but she couldn't help it. She just didn't have the heart to be angry. She told herself he'd already been through enough. But it was more than that. She couldn't have put it into words. This sudden cheeriness in her son's demeanor seemed to carry her back somehow. Back to a faraway and forgotten place and time.

"Watch this," said Chess. He bit a hole out of the middle of two slices of pizza and put them over his eyes, covering the bruises. "Any improvement?"

"Much," laughed Charlotte. Then, without warning, her eyes filled with tears.

At first Chess was oblivious and added, "Think this is how Zorro got started?" He lowered the pizza as he realized she was crying. He felt terrible. "Was it something I said?"

"No," said Charlotte apologetically. "It's just . . . the season."

Chess got the impression he should have understood what this meant. Since he didn't have a clue, he asked, "What's wrong with the season? It's Christmas! I thought you people were always happy at Christmas."

Charlotte raised an eyebrow. "You people?"

"I mean *us* people. You know. Families."

She closed one of her hands around his and used her other hand to tenderly brush the hair out of his face. "You need another haircut. Goodness, it's only been a week! Your hair is growing like ivy."

Chess gazed into her eyes, relishing the attention. She really loved her son. He *felt* it. A lump came into his throat. All his life he'd tried to imagine what it might be like to sit alone with his mother. They wouldn't have had to do anything special. Just talk. Much like this lady was talking to him now. Suddenly he felt self-conscious. He pulled back slightly and looked away. But he couldn't withdraw his hand. It was as if it was cemented in place under hers. He grew angry at himself as a tear streaked his cheek.

Now what have I done? he thought. This display would only inspire more suspicions. It could mess up everything.

But Charlotte took his other hand and squeezed them both gently. He studied her expression. It was one of pure understanding. He couldn't believe it. It was as if she comprehended all of his years of loneliness and rejection, understood perfectly the pain of unbelonging, the heartache of sharing a lifetime of dreams and sorrows with a blank wall. She understood it all, and he didn't have to explain a single word. How was this possible? He wouldn't have thought that anyone in this world could ever understand a heart like his.

It struck him that he should come clean right now, confess everything, and put a stop to this ridiculous charade. But he was powerless to do it. The feeling emanating from this woman's gaze held him fixed. There was no escape.

That afternoon, Charlotte accompanied him to play rehearsal at Eastmont High School. His part was only six lines—two as short as "Er?" and "Hallo!" He was playing the small boy standing below Scrooge's window on Christmas morning—the one sent off to buy the prize turkey that would garnish Bob Cratchit's table. Jordan Holiday, who happened to employ the director's husband, heard that they were looking for grade-school kids to play Tiny Tim and others. He suggested Artemus.

The director, Mrs. Svetson, felt Artie was too tall to play Tiny Tim. But the part of the street boy—the *second* biggest speaking part for grade-schoolers— was just right. Artemus had protested at first, but a bribe from his mother for a new Kitty Hawk model airplane remote cinched the deal.

The costume lady handed Chess a farcical-looking outfit with nylon stockings, puffy cap, and shoes with buckles the size of pancake spatulas. "You've gotta be kidding me," he said to her.

She pursed her lips and commanded, "Dress and meet the director on the proscenium in five minutes."

He felt totally ridiculous sitting in the theater with two dozen other suckers, all dressed in equally ludicrous outfits, while Mrs. Svetson gave them a pep talk about the importance of pulling off a successful dress rehearsal. When she noticed Chess's black eyes, she looked outraged at first. Then she thought about it.

Boy from the street. Loitering below Scrooge's window. Finally she declared, "Works for me."

The dress rehearsal went off without a hitch. That is, until Chess was thrust out from the wings to deliver his lines. Throughout the rehearsal, he'd secretly hoped his part entailed nothing more than standing there, like a piece of scenery. However, as the high-school kid playing Ebenezer Scrooge called down to him, "What's today, my fine fellow?" he merely stood there with his mouth dangling and his knees doing the funky chicken.

A prompt from the wings whispered, "Your line is, *'Today? Why, Christmas Day!'* "

"Today? Why, Christmas Day," Chess repeated with all the enthusiasm of a fence post.

The prompt had to similarly feed him all of his other lines. Afterwards, Mrs. Svetson railed on him big time. "What happened up there, Artemus? I'm freaking out!"

"Just got tongue-tied, I guess."

"Tongue-tied? *Tongue-tied?* If you don't get that knot out of your tongue in the next twenty-four hours, you're gonna look like a blithering idiot. We're *both* gonna look like blithering idiots! Now go home and go over those lines fifty times! Put them on a tape recorder and listen to them in your sleep! Do you hear me?"

"Yes, ma'am."

She made Charlotte promise to enforce this command. During the ride home, Charlotte asked Chess in all sincerity, "Artie, are you okay?"

Chess continued to squirm. Mrs. Svetson was right. He *was* a blithering idiot. A blithering idiot to think he could just slip into another person's life, and everything would be hunky-dory. He didn't even know his sister's first name! He didn't know his own address or phone number! He couldn't have said where he was born or where he'd gone on vacation last summer or who his best friend was!

Calm down, he told himself. *Just take it a moment at a time. One moment at a time.*

"I'm fine, Mom," he answered. "I guess with all those lights and stuff shinin' at me . . ."

"I can help you memorize your lines," said Charlotte, "but I don't know what to do about your stage fright."

"I wasn't scared," Chess said defensively. "I ain't afraid of nothin'."

"You *aren't* afraid of *anything,*" Charlotte corrected. "Goodness, Artie! Did you forget how to speak English overnight?"

"I *aren't* afraid of anything," he repeated. Charlotte slapped his shoulder playfully.

When they got home, the table was littered with cartons of Chinese food. The father and sister had just started serving themselves seconds. Jordan greeted them. "Hey, guys! Don't worry. We saved you the scraps."

As Chess ate his chicken chow mein, he basked in the simple joy of listening to a family conversation. The sister, whose name he'd finally learned was Amber, complained about a boy in her class named Clifford Durfee who'd made it no secret that he had an incurable crush on her, although she didn't like him one little bit. Jordan said the refrigerator was making strange noises and ought to be checked. Charlotte finally brought up the fight at school. Jordan lectured him on the importance of talking things out or deferring to a higher authority before resorting to violence. He listened in awe. He was actually being chewed out by a father! Who'd have imagined that such an experience could actually be *enjoyable*? He relished every minute, promising to follow each bit of corny advice to the letter.

He spent the rest of the evening going over his lines with Jordan and Charlotte. They wondered how he'd forgotten his British accent so fast. But Chess was quick to recover. After all, his last foster parents were movie-musical fanatics. He'd been forced to sit through *My Fair Lady* seven times.

Before bed, the family was called together in the parents' bedroom. Chess watched as everyone dropped to their knees around the king-sized bed.

They looked at him, wondering why he wasn't doing the same.

"Let's go, Artie," said Jordan. "It's your turn."

His spine went rigid. "*My* turn?"

"Yeah, let's go."

"You sure it's my turn?" He pointed at Amber. " 'Cause I think it's *her* turn."

"Sorry, bucko," said Amber.

"Let's not go through this again," said Charlotte. "It's a *privilege* to say prayers, not a punishment."

Awkwardly, Chess lowered down on one knee, then the other. He folded his arms and closed his eyes, mimicking the others. He couldn't recall a single instance when he'd uttered a prayer to anyone or anything in his entire life. He hadn't the foggiest idea what to say. *This could be the final straw,* he decided. In two seconds, they'd all know he was a fraud.

He opened his eyelids a slit and noticed Amber watching him. He caught Jordan opening one eye as well.

He couldn't procrastinate any longer. He pinched his eyes tightly and cleared his throat. "Dear God . . ." After a long pause he added, "God bless us, every one. . . ."

A cold drip of perspiration weaved its way down the back of his neck.

" . . . O bless us God," he continued in a singsong

tone. "Bless everybody who needs to be blessed . . . and we all do need it. A blessing, that is. Bless my mom. Bless my dad. Bless my sister, um . . . Amber . . . Bless me, and . . . and that's it. Unless you can think of somebody else, God. If so, go ahead and bless them, too. Amen."

Chess opened his eyes. He didn't have to look up to know that everybody was gawking at him. Without making eye contact with a single soul, he shot up from his knees and fled the bedroom. "Good night. I'm really tired. Good night."

The others stayed on their knees.

Finally, Jordan declared, "Well, that was . . ." An adjective just didn't come to mind.

Amber dragged herself to her feet. "I know *I* feel blessed. Don't you?"

"Not funny," said her mother.

After Amber left, the parents remained by the bed. Jordan stared off into space. At last he said, "You know what, honey? I *do* feel blessed."

A smile climbed Charlotte's cheeks. She embraced her husband and kissed him.

"You know what?" she said. "So do I."

Ten

❦

ARTEMUS AWAKENED FOR the second time when he heard a key jostling in the lock of the motel room. His heart froze. He pressed against the headboard of the bed, unable to breathe.

The door squeaked on its rusty hinges, and the room was immediately filled with light. But it wasn't daylight. It was the light of a million multi-colored bulbs and neon signs from a skyline of casinos. Standing in the doorway was an ominous silhouette. Artemus braced himself. The predator had returned. The man who'd kidnapped him was back to finish him off.

And yet the man didn't appear to be overly concerned with Artemus's presence as he threw on the light switch. Artemus took in the man's face. It was taut and pointed. Artemus might have guessed he was fifty, although his true age was only thirty-five. He sat on the opposite bed and smiled at Artemus.

"Well, look who's up. How ya' doin', boy?"

Artemus remained frozen and speechless. He realized that his sense of time and place had been fully restored; otherwise, how could he have felt so terrified? Who *was* this villain? What did he want?

The man repeated, "I asked, how are ya feelin'?"

Artemus tried to form a reply, but his lips quivered badly and the only sound that came out was, "Who-who-who—?"

"Who-who-who," the man repeated mockingly. "What's the matter, Chess? You turn into an owl while I was out?"

The words gasped out. "Wh-who are you?"

The man's eyes became thin and scrutinizing. "Who *am* I? You kiddin' me, Chess? You don't know who I am?" He moved toward Artemus, who scrambled to the far side of the bed. "You're joshin' me, ain't ya? You really don't know who I am? It's *me*, kid. Your good buddy, Uncle Boone." He waved his hand in front of Artemus's face. "Can you see okay?"

"What am I doing here?" Artemus demanded, failing to hide a screech in his voice.

"What are *you* doin'? *You* ain't doin' squat. I been doing everything while you been snoozin' like a princess. Now snap out of it, Chess. We got work to do. My luck ain't been so good this time around. I was up nearly $300 around four o'clock, then the ol' Boone Folsom whammy hit. I lost it all. Barely saved enough to afford another night in this dive. We still got four rings left. We're gonna have to slip on up to North Vegas in the morning and find a park. Understand? Don't let me down, Chess. I need you to be sharp as a tack."

"Why do you keep calling me that?"

"Calling you what?"

"That name."

"*Chess?* 'Cause that's your name, dingbat!"

Suddenly it hit Boone what had happened. His eyes widened. He stepped back and clasped his palm to his forehead. "Oh, man. Ohhh, man." He walked back and forth, never taking his eyes off Artemus, sizing him up like a circus freak. "I don't believe it. That knock to your head was worse than I thought. Ohhhh, man. Chess, you better not be foolin' with me. If I find out you're jokin' around, I'll kick the tar outa you from here to Christmas. You really don't know who I am?"

Artemus crinkled his brow. What was this lunatic saying? He thought Artemus was somebody else! *What in blazes was going on?*

"I don't know what you're talking about," Artemus insisted. "My name is not Chess, and you're not my uncle. Take me home. You take me home this minute, or I'll have the cops here so fast—"

Boone laughed. "*Home?* Boy, you *do* have it bad, Chess. You ain't had a home since you was knee-high to a pygmy."

"My name is Artemus Holiday! I live at 3496 South Glendora Court, Salt Lake City, Utah! My dad is Jordan Holiday. My phone number is 801-279-5604. Now I *demand* to know why you've brought me here!"

Boone became genuinely dumbfounded. This was far worse than a case of amnesia. The kid had taken on a whole new *identity*!

"Slow down, boy," said Boone. "Just sloooow down. Start at the beginning. Let's go back to last night. What do you remember?"

"Nothing," said Artemus. "I was chasing that kid, and then . . . I was hit—"

"Hold on. Go back. You was chasin' *who*?"

"That kid! The one who stole my pants and my coat."

A peculiar notion itched under Boone's skin. His sense of logic and reality were crumbling. "That was *you*, Chess. *You* was the one bein' chased."

Artemus shuddered in frustration. "I think I'd know who was chasing who!"

Boone moved in closer, squinting. His hand reached under the lampshade and pressed the switch. With the aid of additional light, his eyes crawled over every contour of the boy's face. Except for the black and blue lump on the kid's forehead, there were no other visible scrapes or bruises. The disparity in the hair caught his attention first. So even. Nearly an inch shorter than his memory of how it had been. It was also his eyes. The shape was just a little . . . And his chin! Where was the—?

He clutched the boy's hair and dragged him closer. "Owww!" Artemus cried, but the assault left him too shocked to resist.

Boone slid his fingers, greasy with the smell of coins from playing slot machines, against the underside of Artemus's chin.

It wasn't there! The scar wasn't there! It was a short scar; anyone else might have missed it. But not Boone. After all, he'd put it there personally by throwing an ashtray at the kid. He knew exactly where that scar should have been. And it wasn't *there*.

Boone released him roughly. "What did you say your name was?"

His teeth were chattering. "A-Artemus. Artemus Holiday."

"Your address?"

"It's 3496 South Glendora Court, Salt Lake City, Utah, 84—"

"Shut up." Boone began pacing, his eyes wild, his

teeth gnawing at a dirty thumbnail. How could this have happened? What had become of Chess?

There was only one possibility. Chess *was* the person taken away in that ambulance. And if Boone was stupid enough to mistake this boy for Chess, might it also be possible that . . . ? His mind conjured all the grimmest ramifications. It was kidnapping, pure and simple. This boy was a magnet for cops. Soon there'd be a missing-child poster on the desk of every policeman in the country. What was worse, the kid had seen him. If he escaped, he was sure to finger Boone. That might enable the police to pick up his trail. Even standing in the same room with him was like standing with one foot inside a prison cell. Boone had sworn he'd never go back to jail. He'd take his own life before anyone caged him up again. What should he do? He needed time to think.

Artemus cowered against the headboard, stiff with fear. He could still feel the slimy touch of the man's fingers against his flesh. He fully expected the man to kill him at any moment. He thought about the lessons his mother had tried to hammer into his skull all during his childhood—lessons about avoiding strangers and eluding abductors. Once she'd made him repeat certain rules of conduct if an abductor had you cornered. He'd told himself she was just paranoid, and he'd learned to block her out.

Forgive me, Mom, he cried in his heart. *I can't remember a single rule.*

"I want to go home," he pleaded.

"Yeah," said Boone absently. "Absolutely. Home."

Maybe that was *the best idea,* thought Boone. Just drive the kid home. Drop him off on some interstate outside of Salt Lake City. Let him walk to town while he turned the car around and made tracks to the nearest state line. Then it occurred to him—*Oh, man!* He'd already told the kid his name! What a mess! Could anything have screwed up his life worse than this? He looked into the child's frightened eyes. He felt no pity. His own situation had become far more desperate.

"Just let me go," said Artemus. "I-I won't tell anyone."

"No!" Boone shrieked. Letting him go was not an option. If he got away now, Boone might never get out of Vegas. He calmed himself and said, "Just look at you, kid. You got one sock. No shoes. The tags are still on those pants. You know how many weirdos there are in this town? How far do you think you'd get?"

"Please," said Artemus softly. "Don't hurt me."

Boone sugarcoated his voice. "Now, why would I do that? Tell you what. I'll take you home myself. You know, this is all a crazy misunderstanding."

"You'll take me home now?"

"Right now."

Artemus stiffened as Boone approached. He closed his eyes as Boone grabbed his arm, certain the end had come.

"Come on," said Boone. "I'm takin' you to the car." With a grip tight enough to squeeze off the circulation, Boone led Artemus to the door. The Buick was parked right outside.

"I-I don't want a ride," said Artemus. "I—I'd rather—"

"What's the matter, kid? Trust me. Get in the car."

Artemus was hauled to the Buick's rear door. Boone forced him inside, almost slamming the door on the kid's neck. Then he stood there a moment and surveyed the surroundings. It was almost midnight. Las Vegas was just picking up steam. Pedestrians moved in a steady stream along the sidewalk, but they were way on the other side of the street, a good fifty yards distant. For the moment, the motel's parking area was clear. This was good. He needed a minute of privacy.

He remembered some twine in the trunk. He could truss up the boy's hands and feet and lay him on the floor in the backseat. This would insure that the kid wouldn't do anything unexpected, at least not until Boone was good and ready to let him go. Or, if Boone opted to resolve this problem in an entirely different manner . . . perhaps similar to the way he'd

89

resolved a certain problem in Florida . . . well, he'd have time to contemplate that as well.

He popped the trunk. The twine was tangled up in the car jack. He untangled as much as he thought he'd need, winding it into an unassuming ball. As he reapproached the back door, he attempted to hide it behind his back.

Artemus fidgeted in the backseat, his heart banging like a kettledrum. *Run!* his instincts clamored. *Get away while you can!* Terror glued him to the seat. He licked his lips, working up the nerve. His hand was just about to spring for the door handle when Boone reopened it. Artemus looked into his eyes. Cold and determined. He held something behind his back. Boone leaned in, and the twine was revealed.

"Give me your hands," he gruffed. "And I'm warning you, if you yell I'll—"

Something in the boy's frozen psyche shattered. Boone's threats no longer paralyzed him. He wrenched out a cry and scrambled to the other side of the Buick, flailing his arms. Boone leaned in farther and fought desperately to catch one of his wrists and get a knot around it. Artemus found the latch of the door handle. He propelled himself out onto the pavement by placing his foot on Boone's face and shoving off.

Boone lunged one final time. The lunge left him

hanging headfirst out of the vehicle, arms and neck tangled in twine.

Bristling with terror, pulsing with adrenaline, Artemus shot across the motel parking lot, rounding the cinder-block barrier that separated the motel from a wedding chapel next door. He'd covered a full city block before he dared to look back. Boone was nowhere in sight. And now there were pedestrians all around him. A kidnapper wouldn't dare try anything here. He had to stop someone. He had to ask for help—maybe the lady in the sequined halter top, or the man in the leather vest. No one was even paying attention to him. Here he was, panting like a racehorse, barefoot, one sock—and no one was even curious? Didn't anything in this town qualify as unusual?

Still breathless and panicked, he approached a young couple walking arm in arm, oogling into each other's eyes. "Help!" he cried. "There's a guy after me!"

The man reluctantly looked at Artemus. "What's the matter, kid?"

"This man! He's trying to kidnap me!"

"Where? I don't see anyone."

"He's at that motel!" He pointed toward the half-hidden sign of the Lampluster Motel.

"Looks like you're safe now," said the man.

"But—"

The lady laid her inch-long fingernails on his shoulders. "Oh, he's so *cuuuute*! But maybe you better go home, sweetie. Your mom might be worried."

Artemus shrugged her off. What a ditz! Did she think this was a joke? He pushed past them.

"Good luck, kid!"

Artemus ambled through the pulsing casino lights, intermingled now and then with gaudy Christmas decorations. He passed beneath a giant animated marquee featuring Santa Claus winning big at a slot machine. He checked his back again and again. He needed to find a phone. Call his parents. They must be going psycho by now. Had the kidnapper demanded a ransom? Was his father even now scraping together every last cent they owned to get him back? Where was a policeman when you needed one?

At a casino entrance, he spotted a man in a uniform. A cop? A security guard? *Please,* thought Artemus. *Please be someone who'll help me.*

He approached the man. "Are you a policeman?"

"Just a doorman. You lookin' for a cop?"

Artemus nodded.

"The Metro is right over there." He pointed toward a tall semicircular building down the block.

"The *Metro*?" asked Artemus.

"The police station. The cop shop. What's the problem?" He glanced at the boy's feet and grinned. "Someone steal your shoes?"

92

Artemus ignored the question and started toward the semicircular building, first at a brisk walk, then at a run. Stepping off the curb, he drenched his remaining sock in the rain gutter. He stripped it off and tossed it aside. He crossed the street and continued up the sidewalk, soon entering the central plaza of the Las Vegas Metropolitan Police Department.

There were several entrances and doorways, but only one had a light burning. As he pushed his way inside, a wave of relief washed over him. He'd made it! He was safe! He'd be on the phone with his parents in five minutes or less!

The desk sergeant was situated behind a thick glass partition, conversing with a fat man in a T-shirt that featured a gorilla drinking two kegs of beer simultaneously. The caption read, PARTY ANIMAL. Behind the man was a short black lady with her teenage daughter.

Artemus was hesitant at first. What was his next step? Should he charge up to the front and cry, "Help! I've been kidnapped!"? He didn't have the nerve, so he simply got in line. What else could he do? No, he'd just wait his turn, like everyone else.

The desk sergeant, a grim-looking man with a mustache, listened with calculated indifference as the first man in line jabbered on and on about how his old girlfriend had vandalized his car and sprayed obscene graffiti on his driveway. The sergeant repeated three times that he couldn't press charges without an eyewitness or some other evidence. Cussing, the man finally left.

The black lady wanted to know what they could do about a neighbor boy who'd threatened her daughter with bodily harm. Artemus waited, biting his fingernails to the bone, growing more distressed by the minute. Surely his case took priority over these people's. He'd been *abducted*, for heaven's sake!

At last, his turn arrived. He stepped up to the tiny grill hole in the glass.

The sergeant took a bite out of his sandwich. He chewed and swallowed before finally inquiring, "What can I do for you?"

"I've been kidnapped," said Artemus.

"What's that?"

"I've been kidnapped."

"Kidnapped?" he repeated skeptically. "By who?"

"A man in a motel. I got away."

"What's your name?"

"Artemus. Artemus Holiday."

"Where do you live, Artemus?"

"Salt Lake City."

"Utah? You mean a man abducted you in Salt Lake City and drove you to Las Vegas?"

"Yes."

94

"And then you got away?"

"Yes."

The man finally took enough interest to set down his sandwich. He slid his chair over to a computer terminal.

"Spell your name for me."

Artemus did so. The officer punched it into the computer and waited. "Doesn't come up. How long ago were you kidnapped?"

"Yesterday . . . I think."

"You *think*? Did your abductor hit you on the head?"

"I don't think so."

"How'd you get that bump?"

"A car, I think. I-I'm not sure."

"You don't know where you got that bump?"

"It was a truck. It happened just before I was kidnapped."

The sergeant studied Artemus carefully. He sucked a piece of food out of his teeth. "Are your parents in Las Vegas?"

"No. They're in Salt Lake."

"Do they know you're missing?"

"Of *course* they know," he snapped. "What do you think?"

"It's just that it hasn't been reported. This terminal networks the entire—"

"I don't care what your computer says! *I was kidnapped!*"

"All right," said the sergeant. "Calm down. What's your phone number?"

He recited it hastily. The sergeant wrote it down. "And that's a Salt Lake number?"

"Criminy! What do you think I've been telling you?"

"Have a seat on the bench."

"Are you gonna call? Can I talk to them?"

"Just have a seat."

Artemus clenched his teeth. The last thing he wanted to do was sit. He wanted to talk to his parents! He stepped back as if to move toward the bench, then he pressed up against the glass again. The sergeant went to a phone along the back counter.

Artemus curled and uncurled his toes as the sergeant dialed his number. *Thirty more seconds,* he thought. *Thirty more seconds, and this nightmare will be over.*

The sergeant watched Artemus thoughtfully, almost ruefully, as he waited for the other party to pick up. As someone answered, his eyes turned away. Artemus couldn't hear too well through the glass. He tried to read the sergeant's lips. He thought he heard, *"I've got a kid here who claims . . ."*—but then the sergeant turned his back completely.

Artemus waited. The sergeant took forever. Why didn't he bring the phone over? A chill ran through him. Something wasn't right. Had the sergeant dialed the wrong number? What was he saying? Why wasn't there some indication of glee, or at least satisfaction at having just solved a major case? The sergeant's demeanor seemed to grow more serious and sullen. *Why won't he let me talk to them? They're my parents, for crying out loud!*

Artemus rapped impatiently on the glass. What kind of police station was this? They wouldn't let a kid who'd been abducted talk to his parents? To his utter mortification, the sergeant hung up the phone. He faced Artemus with a punitive gaze.

"What's going on?" Artemus called through the grill hole. "Why won't you let me talk to them?"

"Why don't you tell me what's *really* going on, son?"

"*What are you talking about?* I've told you—!"

"They don't know who you are, kid. Let's start from the beginning."

Artemus was beside himself. "Start over? *I wanna talk to my parents!*"

"You and I both know those aren't your parents."

"You're crazy! Did you dial 801–279—?"

"Don't worry. I dialed it. A Mr. Jordan Holiday."

"That's my dad! I'm his son!"

"Mr. Holiday's children are all present and accounted for. Nobody's been kidnapped. Now, let's start with your real name and where you're from."

The boy exploded. "My name is Artemus Holiday! What's wrong with you people? Call him back! Call him back *now*! I want to talk to him!"

"I'm not waking up anybody else in the middle of the night. Now, if you're not gonna give me your real name—"

"Don't you get it? *I've been kidnapped!*"

"Then why don't you tell me your *abductor's* name?"

"Boone," said Artemus. "Boone Folsom. Or Folsom Boone. Something like that. He's at the Lampluster Motel *right now*! Or at least he was. He was trying to *hurt* me!"

"Wait right there," said the sergeant. He made his way to the exit door that led out into the foyer.

Artemus trembled uncontrollably. Why would his father tell the sergeant that all his children were present and accounted for? Had the world gone *insane*? The man on the phone was *not* his father! It was an impostor! Someone was lying! They'd abducted his whole family! It was a conspiracy! What was happening to him? Tears sprang from his eyes.

The desk sergeant took him by the shoulder. "Come back here with me, son."

"I wanna talk to my dad! Why won't you call him back? I wanna talk to my mom!"

"Just follow me."

He followed reflexively, mindlessly, his vision blurred by hysteria. His world was spinning into a void of blackness. Everything he'd always taken for granted—security, love, sanctuary, and a sense of belonging—had become as fleeting as frost on a summer morning.

Jordan returned to his bedroom from the darkened hallway. The portable phone from the night table was still in his hand. He set it back in place.

"What was that all about?" Charlotte asked sleepily.

"Weird," said Jordan. "That was the Las Vegas police."

"Police?" said Charlotte with alarm.

"Some sergeant in Las Vegas wondered if I was missing any children."

"Missing? Why would he think that?"

"He said there was a kid at his desk claiming to have been kidnapped. The kid gave the police our number."

"Did you check the bedrooms?"

"Of course," said Jordan. "All sound asleep. I told him he must have the wrong family. Or the wrong number. He sounded really embarrassed."

"Las Vegas?"

"That's what the guy said."

"Weird," said Charlotte.

"Yeah." Jordan slipped back into bed.

"I hope they straighten it out."

"So do I," he said, fighting a yawn.

After a few minutes, Charlotte whispered again, "Really weird."

She wasn't sure why she couldn't seem to get back to sleep for the remainder of the night.

Eleven

❦

"TELL ME SOMETHING, Mom," Chess said to Charlotte that morning at breakfast. It surprised even him how easily "Mom" and "Dad" now came to his lips. "How come we hardly got any Christmas decorations?"

Chess knew he might be treading on thin ground by interfering with family custom. But after last night, he'd started to believe he might be infallible. He could do or say anything; it didn't matter. His membership in this family was inextricable. After eleven years of loneliness and chaos, the gods of destiny were finally smiling down. As a result, Chess Folsom was determined to live to the fullest every fantasy every orphan had ever craved. At the top of his list was a full-blown, no-holds-barred family Christmas extravaganza.

CHRIS HEIMERDINGER

However, to his consternation, his question only seemed to have caused a rather uncomfortable hush.

"What do you mean?" Charlotte replied uneasily, stalling in hopes that someone might change the subject. No one came to the rescue.

"I mean, look at this place," said Chess. "You call that a Christmas tree? How come we don't go out and get a *real* tree? And real Christmas lights— *hundreds* of 'em. I bet we could do up the place twice as good as anybody else in this neighborhood. We could create a light show bright enough to be seen from the moon!"

Chess could feel the mood in the room growing tense, but he chose to ignore it. How could such a subject possibly be the cause of any distress?

"Well, son," said Jordan. "You know that we've never really been . . . you know, the type to—"

"How come?" he persisted. "Everybody in the whole town—the whole *world!*—is getting into the Christmas spirit. What's the matter with *us*?"

Amber cleared her throat. "Maybe Artie's right," she said meekly. "Maybe . . . it's time."

"What do you mean *maybe*?" Chess raved. "Of *course* it's time! I say after this play thing tonight, we all come home and throw a party. Light a fire. Drink eggnog. Sing Christmas carols. The whole nine yards. I mean . . . it's what families do, right?" He looked

102

from Jordan to Charlotte and back again. "What do you say?"

"We'll think about it, Artie," said Jordan.

"What's there to think about? Let's *do* it!"

Jordan nodded. "We'll think about it."

Jordan was still thinking about it an hour later as he waited in a traffic jam on I-15. It had snowed again last night, and the storm was still under way. Morning commuters had apparently forgotten what it was like to drive on Utah highways in December. Various emergency vehicles zipped past him in the outside lane. He had no idea how far up the highway the accident was situated, or how long he would be delayed.

The wiper beat at a steady rhythm. As he watched the blade flick back and forth, his mind drifted back to that fateful day eight years before. At first he fought it; such tormenting images were usually reserved for the interstices of night, when he was too weak to stop them. It was day now; he was conscious and strong. He should have been able to turn the images off. But his will relented. To his dismay, a floodgate opened. The dreadful memories raged in his thoughts like a cyclone, blazing with more clarity than ever before.

It had been a much snowier December that particular year, a much snowier Christmas. Far more delays had been generated on the highways. Sidewalks just wouldn't stay shoveled, and the snowplows had buried his car twice at his place of business. Nevertheless, despite the weather, Jordan Holiday was on top of the world.

His software business had successfully launched a national product line. It was his first overwhelming success in over four years of financial headaches and disappointments. Almost overnight, the money started pouring into his bank accounts. For the first time in his young married life, he and his wife Charlotte, along with their five-year-old daughter, Amber, and their three-year-old twins, Artemus and Andrew, would enjoy the sweet bliss of financial success. And best of all, they would enjoy it at Christmas.

Jordan's first order of business that winter was to purchase the house of his dreams. He was not a materialistic man by nature. He would have balked at the desire to own boats or sports cars or other luxury toys. But he did have one weakness: he'd always dreamed of owning an enormous house on a sizable chunk of land. There were at least two dozen specifics that he and Charlotte had mapped out together. The home they finally settled on, located at the southern end of the valley, fulfilled every last detail—including Jordan's ultimate indulgence of having their property line extend to the banks of the Jordan River, a section that was teeming with freshly stocked rainbow trout. He envisioned a life where he'd awaken at sunrise and have trout frying in a pan before work.

That year, Jordan and Charlotte tried to make Christmas morning a child's ultimate fantasy. When the ritual of opening presents had concluded, the living room looked like a wasteland of wrapping paper and ribbons. But despite all the expensive gifts that their twin sons had piled into two corners of the room, the one that surprisingly captured their attention more than any other was a pair of Styrofoam gliders, retailing at about $6.95. Even before breakfast, Charlotte found herself bundling the three-year-olds in mittens, scarves, and matching "Attack Force" leather jackets so they could give their new toys a test flight in the field to the side of the house.

Jordan was busily frying bacon when his wife suggested that he check on them.

"Just a second," he replied, and made sure that each strip was carefully turned to the other side.

He was wearing only a T-shirt and jogging pants when he stepped out onto the back porch and began calling their names. Neither boy responded. Jordan looked around. They were nowhere to be seen. He was about to make his way around to the front yard when it struck him that a small boy might consider it a far more enticing prospect to launch his airplane from the lip of the hill overlooking the river. Grumbling, he trudged fifty yards to its edge. The snow was made blindingly white by the morning sun and cloudless sky. When he reached the overlook and stared down into the river valley, his blood turned cold.

"Andrew!" he cried. "Don't move! Stay where you are!"'

After the boy had launched his plane from the lip of the hill, the glider had landed on a shelf of ice that extended out over the river. Artemus now stood on the bank with his airplane in hand, watching innocently as Andrew forged his way out onto the shelf to retrieve his toy.

It was as if Jordan's voice had created the final vibration in the air—the final shock wave that encouraged the shelf to crack. He was still stumbling down the hill at a full run when Andrew, submerged in freezing water up to the shoulders of his leather jacket, began screaming for help.

"Don't move!" Jordan cried a second time as his son dug his fingernails into the last clinging section of the ice shelf.

"Daddy!" Andrew cried.

"Get your mother!" Jordan shouted back at Artemus. "Tell her to call 911! Understand? 911!"

The horrified father lay down on the ice shelf and squirmed his way out to where the three-year-old fought to maintain a grip against the current. Jordan was almost there—just inches from grasping his son's sleeve—when the final chunk broke free.

"Daddy! Help me! Help—!"

The river immediately sucked him under. The look of horror on his child's face seared its terrible brand onto Jordan's mind. The current dragged his son's helpless body beneath a wider, thicker shelf of ice that nearly crossed the entire breadth of the river. Jordan screamed Andrew's name and scrambled to the far edge of the ice shelf—about fifteen feet away—waiting desperately for the current to carry him out, ready to pluck him from the slushy swell. The current was strong; it should have only been a few seconds. Three or four eternal seconds!

The boy did not reappear.

"Andyyyyy!"

Still wearing only his T-shirt and jogging pants, Jordan plunged headlong into the murky depths. He swam upcurrent, underneath the shelf. The current carried him out, but he dove back under again and again, screaming his son's name. The blue pallor of frostbite started sinking into his marrow. The adrenaline that had kept his body warm started to dissipate. His head grew light. His muscles stiffened. The current began to carry him at will. He realized that his own circumstances had become as dire as his son's, but he didn't care. The crush of grief was

107

unbearable. That look in his son's eyes! It was better to die. Better to drown than face the excruciating pain.

And then he heard the whisper, or at least he thought he heard it, rising faintly above the rush of water in his ears, tinkling almost like a windchime in a summer breeze: *"It's all right, Daddy. I'm not cold anymore. I'm not cold anymore."*

Jordan wedged himself in the branches of a fallen tree. He hung there, still submerged up to his armpits, his flesh lifeless and numb, his only source of warmth the tears that scorched his cheeks. It was there that Jordan lost consciousness, there that he forever lost a portion of his soul.

Artemus had remained in the snow at the top of the hill. He just didn't have the strength to tear his eyes away from the horrible scene. The tiny child was still paralyzed with shock when his mother found him. From that day on, he was fully aware that he had failed. Failed to reach his mother. Failed to deliver his father's message. Failed to save his brother's life. This was the mantra that a three-year-old boy would carry in his subconscious for the rest of his life.

A score of searchers dredged the river for miles downstream, but there was just too much ice. Too many secret places where the body might lodge itself. It was spring before Andrew's body was finally recovered, still wearing the faded and mud-crusted "Attack Force" jacket.

After the accident, Jordan spent three days in the hospital recovering from hypothermia. When the new year dawned, the first task of the shattered family was to sell their dream home on the banks of the Jordan River. Even before the body was recovered, the Holidays purchased a plot in a nearby cemetery and erected a memorial to Andrew's memory. Then finally, on a warm March morning, Andrew's body was laid to rest in the earth, its peace never to be disturbed again. It was on that morning that a grief-crippled Charlotte Holiday laid the first white gardenia at the monument, an event faithfully repeated every month for the past eight years.

Not only did they bury a son in the graveyard that year. They buried the spirit of Christmas. In the years to come, for the sake of their two remaining children, Jordan and Charlotte had attempted to go through the motions, but it soon became apparent that no one was very enthusiastic. There was too much pain associated with that day. Too much misery dredged up by all of the rituals—even for the children. Not even the recollection of that Being whose birthday Christmas was instituted to celebrate had been able to heal them of their grief. And for a family whose lives were as devoted to their Savior and to their faith as the Holidays, this may have been the most painful fact of all. The healing power of Him who had healed the world could not be embraced by them on the one day that it should have been most penetrating.

As the years trudged on, Jordan accepted the fact that never again would their living room be a joyful wasteland of wrapping paper and ribbons. He'd grown comfortable in his belief that there would never again be tinsel or carols or other fanfare. At most, the family would erect a modest artificial tree, and exchange one or two meager gifts. This is how it had been for the last eight years, and this is how it would always be.

That was why the things his son had said that morning bothered him so deeply. The boy's suggestion that they break with the established pattern and throw some sort of Christmas celebration had forced him to relive all the dark events that had brought them to this place in time. Artemus should have known better. What was worse, Artemus had Amber— and even his wife!—supporting the suggestion. Charlotte had gone so far as to make definite plans to take them both after school to purchase a real Christmas tree—ten feet tall with all the trimmings. A knot tightened in Jordan's chest as he thought about it.

He wondered why he should feel so threatened by the idea. Was it wrong that his son—the one whom therapists had claimed would be most adversely affected by the event—should be the one to lead the way to renewal and recovery? Perhaps all his family needed was a cue from one of its members. Could he take the cue from Artemus? For thirty years prior to Andrew's death, Jordan's memories of Christmas had always been joyful and bright. Why had he allowed this one single Christmas to blacken the event forever in his mind?

Because I couldn't reach him, Jordan reminded himself. *Because I couldn't save his life. Because of that look in his eyes before the river took him away from me forever.*

As the traffic on I-15 started to inch forward again, his mind careened one last time through all the details of that awful day. As he found himself once again wedged in the branches of that tree, water swirling around his shoulders, he felt the sting of another scorching tear on his cheek.

And then the strangest thing happened. Jordan drew a breath, and his palms tightened around the leather of the steering wheel. An image flashed in his mind—something he'd seen that morning just before he'd blacked out.

How odd, he thought. How odd that he'd forgotten. Even more odd was the fact that his mind seemed so drawn to it now. Why should he remember it now? The reason he'd forgotten it was obvious—it would have seemed so trivial, so insignificant beside such a tragic event. Even now it struck him as little more than a curiosity. Still, he couldn't let it go. He strained until the image came sharply into focus, just as he'd seen it on that fateful morning.

Yes, Jordan thought. *Now I remember it perfectly.*

He became aware that the car behind him was bearing down on its horn. He let up on the brake and continued down the interstate to complete his last day at the office. The last working day before Christmas.

Twelve

THE LONGEST NIGHT in the life of Artemus Holiday was finally over, only to be succeeded, as it appeared, by the longest day.

The police had first taken him to the University Medical Center, where doctors and psychologists poked and prodded, asked questions, and scribbled notes. Their initial diagnosis was that Artemus was delusional, perhaps the host of multiple personalities. How else might they explain a boy who thought he was somebody else?

Around 4:00 A.M. they took him to a place called Child Haven, directly adjacent to the center for juvenile detention. It was a minimum-security facility with low, unbarbed fences, designed as temporary

housing for abused and abandoned children. Artemus, however, knew better. It was nothing less
than a prison. He was a prisoner of the justice system of Las Vegas, Nevada. A prisoner to mindless,
conscienceless zombies. What other description
could suit a circus of people who wouldn't believe a
single word that came out of his mouth?

"Just let me talk to my parents in Salt Lake for
thirty seconds," he tirelessly pleaded. "Then you'll
know that I'm telling the truth. You'll know that I
really am who I say I am."

His vigilance finally earned him a nod of consent
from one of the directors at Child Haven, Mr. Pulsipher. "All right," he agreed. "Thirty seconds."

Artemus shuddered with relief. "Now?"

Pulsipher scoffed. "It's 4:00 A.M! I'll let you call in
the morning." He raised a finger of warning. "Remember, though, I'll be listening on the other line.
Now I want you to get some sleep."

Artemus was left in a private room with a cold
tiled floor in the central building of Child Haven's
campus. His nerves remained on edge. He didn't
think he could sleep a wink. After all, he'd been
sleeping for the last two days. For the first hour, he
repeatedly wandered out into the dining and living
area to check the time on the wall clock. Pulsipher
had stated that reveille was promptly at 7:00 A.M. He

fully expected to be speaking on the phone with his mother at 7:05.

Around 6:00 A.M., he lay back on the bedroom's stiff mattress and closed his eyes. The next thing he knew, he was wandering alone through a wind-swept desert. It seemed like days passed. Finally, he came upon a chest filled with treasure. But as he opened the lid, someone pushed him down into it from behind. A key turned in the lock. Trapped! He was surrounded by gold and jewels, yet he was convinced he was suffocating. No one could hear him banging. No one responded to his cries.

Artemus awakened with a start. He sat up. As his eyes fell into focus, he realized that his bed was surrounded by people. Standing inside his room were Mr. Pulsipher, the desk sergeant from the night before, a uniformed guard from the detention center next door, and another man with dark curly hair and an extra-wide tie covered with Roadrunners and Wile E. Coyotes. Everyone wore expressions of stone, except for Pulsipher and the man with dark curly hair. These two persons were smiling, but it wasn't a cheerful smile. It was almost a sneer.

"Good morning," said Pulsipher.

Artemus rubbed his eyes. By the light, he'd have guessed it was much later than 7:00 A.M. It appeared that they'd let him sleep in, perhaps on account of the lateness of his arrival.

Pulsipher introduced the man with curly hair. "This is Detective Quesinhurt. He has some information that I think you'd be very interested in hearing, young man."

"What's that?" asked Artemus groggily.

Quesinhurt stepped forward. He held a piece of paper in front of Artemus's face. "Recognize this man?"

Artemus caught his breath. It was a mug shot of the man from the motel! "That's the guy!" he cried. "That's the one who kidnapped me and drove me to Las Vegas!"

Quesinhurt and the desk sergeant exchanged a congratulatory glance. The sergeant's hunch to try and connect the name of Boone Folsom/Folsom Boone with a known felon had obviously succeeded. But the presentation wasn't over. The detective flashed a second photograph before his eyes.

"And how about this strapping young fellow? Do you recognize him?"

Artemus let the image sink in. The picture showed a smiling boy, nine or ten years old, wearing a wrinkled dress shirt. It looked like a blowup of some sort of cheesy yearbook photo. *Of course!* It was the kid from the clothing store! The one who stole his pants!

"I know him, too!" Artemus declared.

General laughter percolated through the room.

"No kidding," said the detective. "Then maybe you also know that this young fellow has caused quite a stir. That is, since he ran away from the child welfare services in Tallahassee, Florida, about eighteen months ago. Seems he's been on a bit of a crime spree all across the United States with his uncle, Boone Folsom—a man wanted in Florida for murder. That right, son? Or perhaps I should call you Lawrence. Or Chess, if you like. That is the preferred name on your file."

Artemus's head was swimming. "My *file*? You think this is *me*? You're crazy! You're all crazy!"

"Don't make this any more difficult," said the detective. "You're in some serious hot water, son. On the bright side, there's a lot of people who have been very concerned about your whereabouts for a very long time."

"Listen to me! This is *not me*! I can prove it! Let me call my parents!" He turned to Pulsipher. "You promised I could call!"

Pulsipher only shrugged. Artemus started hyperventilating. The nightmare wasn't over at all. It had only *begun*!

Quesinhurt continued. "You'll be remanded into custody in the detention facility next door until the D.A.'s office in Florida can arrange for your extradition. It might take a few days, since it's so close to

Christmas. In the meantime, you would be well advised to cooperate with us in our efforts to apprehend your uncle—"

"No!" Artemus clamored. "My name is not Chess, or Lawrence, or—! Please! You have to listen to me! This is all a horrible mistake!"

The detective sighed and turned to the guard. "Let's get him processed next door before we go any further."

Artemus saw the flash of metal as the guard produced a pair of handcuffs. *Handcuffs!* They were going to lead him away like a common criminal! Panic, rage, and desperation washed over him like tidal waves. His life as he'd known it was over. It had all been stripped away in a blinding flash. Christmas would be spent rotting in a juvenile jail in Nevada! New Year's would be spent under lock and key in Florida! What if he never saw his mother, father, or sister again? Was it possible?

From there, his thought process was instantaneous. Instinct took command. Head down, fists swinging, he bolted toward the door. Pulsipher and the guard tried to block him. As Pulsipher grabbed his shoulder, Artemus put him out of commission with a knee to the groin.

The guard seized his arm, snapping the handcuffs smoothly around his right wrist. Artemus's teeth found the man's thumb. He bit down hard. The guard shrieked and let go. Artemus had reached the doorway, but the desk sergeant was on top of him. He dropped to the floor. The sergeant tripped. The guard, holding his crushed thumb, made a second feeble effort to nab him, but Artemus scrambled across the floor. Upon reaching the dining area, he overturned several flimsy chairs and a small round table to block the attacks of Quesinhurt and the guard. Next, he lunged toward the exit, barely escaping the grasp of three separate pairs of arms. He burst outside. Now, if he could just reach the perimeter fence—

There were children on the lawn. Several arose and actually started cheering, "Go! Go! Go!" He was halfway to freedom, handcuffs still dangling from his right wrist, as Quesinhurt, Pulsipher, and the desk sergeant bumbled out the doorway.

Beyond the five-foot fence was an industrial stockyard with stacks of pipe and giant spools of cable. As he threw himself over the top bar, tearing his sleeve clean away from the rest of his shirt, he felt Quesinhurt's hand groping at his back. But the detective failed to find a grip. Artemus fell into the stockyard.

He was a good hundred feet across the yard before anyone else traversed the fence, shattering any and all records he might have held at his grade school. By the time he conquered a second fence and landed in a city park, most of his pursuers had turned back. They were now scrambling for automobiles or telephones.

Still barefoot and panting heavily, Artemus continued west, crossing a street called Mojave and entering a construction area where the frames of half-built houses painted long, barred shadows. After another minute, his breath spent, his muscles turning to jelly, he entered one of the skeletal homes and found a shaded corner. Dropping to his knees, he heaved for oxygen. As his lungs became satisfied, he broke into sobs.

For now he was free, but to what end? Where did he go from here? He was penniless, shoeless, starving, broken in spirit—a wanted fugitive, and four hundred miles from home. His prospects for the future looked about as dismal as any human being's could ever get. He curled up in the corner. For over an hour, he didn't move. He tried to sort out his thoughts, but his thoughts just wouldn't sort. Not even the moan of sirens moving up and down the neighboring avenues could wake him from his daze. Only one concept resounded: *I want to go home. Please, God, let me go home.*

Beneath the wheels of Boone Folsom's Buick, the lonely miles of southern Utah rolled on.

I'll be in Salt Lake in four hours, he told himself. Shortly thereafter, he hoped the great mystery would be solved. He couldn't afford to take much longer. After filling his tank in Vegas, he had less than fifteen dollars to his name. He'd nearly doubled that money at a mini-market in St. George by asking for change from the teenage cashier. He got the girl so flustered that she handed him two extra fives by mistake. It was an old shell game, but it still worked pretty well.

And yet he knew this penny-ante stuff wouldn't carry him far. He needed his partner back, his good-luck charm. Until now, he hadn't realized how dependent he'd become on the little whelp. It bruised his pride to admit this. But it was a matter of survival. Reluctantly, he put his personal feelings aside.

He had to wonder, what if Chess had gotten himself tangled up with the authorities? Then he smirked to himself. Not ol' Chess. If that boy possessed even half the talent he suspected, the kid was at this very moment reclining in the lap of luxury at the home of Mr. and Mrs. Jordan Holiday on 3496 South Glendora Court.

Or was it 3946? He couldn't quite remember. Not that it mattered. He could confirm the address easily enough with a Salt Lake directory. Boone had allowed a secret hope to creep into his thoughts. He reveled in the possibilities that might await him if this address was located in one of the city's nicer neighborhoods. If so, the situation could become very interesting. It was entirely possible that Chess was sitting right on top of a gold mine—a gold mine just begging to be transferred into the hands of a more deserving and needy soul. Like his, for example.

He realized that such ambitions presented other concerns. What if the sometimes-oblivious Chess decided not to cooperate? Or what if this family of fools decided to put up a fuss? To quell these concerns, Boone's hand massaged the cracking vinyl of the seat beside him. Hidden inside the coils sat his .38 caliber revolver. *Nope,* Boone assured himself. He didn't figure anybody would be giving him too much trouble.

Thirteen

❧

IT WAS DUSK before Artemus finally dared to venture out from his hiding place. The empty pain in his stomach had forced him to act. He hadn't eaten a full meal in almost three days. Except for a few snacks last night at the hospital, he hadn't eaten anything at all. Fortunately, he found a working faucet in the half-built house to slake his thirst; otherwise, he might have shriveled up in the Las Vegas heat, which topped out at nearly eighty degrees despite the fact that it was almost Christmas.

He'd had many hours to contemplate his next move. Nevertheless, very little inspiration had been forthcoming. He'd tried to envision himself breaking into somebody's home and using their phone, but he just couldn't dredge up the courage. It would be just his luck to select a house where he'd awaken a three-hundred-pound sumo wrestler with a shotgun. In the end, he decided to place a collect call to Salt Lake City, Utah. He needed to find a pay phone. He couldn't remember ever having used a pay phone in his entire life. It needed a quarter, right? How difficult could it be to obtain a quarter?

As he ambled down the sidewalk, he hid his hand-cuffed wrist inside his shirt. He remained wary. The juvenile detention facility was still only a few blocks away. He imagined spies peering at him from every window, notifying their comrades by walkie-talkie that the subject had just been sighted—move in for the kill. He wouldn't have been surprised if his escape had been featured on the evening news. The entire city of Las Vegas was probably on the lookout for an eleven-year-old male wearing blue slacks, a torn shirt, no shoes, and a pair of handcuffs dangling from one wrist.

Despite his paranoia, it was a fairly quiet evening. Of the occasional pedestrians and drivers who raised their eyes to look at him, none paid him so much as a second glance. Still, he appreciated the fact that daylight was fading, making him less visible.

He finally turned north, and then east again, always keeping to streets with less traffic. At last he reached a bustling avenue called Lamb. There he found an AM/PM market with a bank of pay phones. Drawing a deep breath, he donned the saddest puppy-dog look he could muster, and approached a lady just hanging up the gas pump.

He cleared his throat. "Hello. I was wondering, if I took your name and address and promised to pay you back, could you loan me a quarter?"

She looked startled, as if Artemus was about to mug her. Were eleven-year-olds habitually known to mug people around here?

"No change," she replied and hopped into her vehicle.

She drove away without looking back. Artemus's face was beet red. Even his desperation couldn't quash the humiliation of having to beg for a mere quarter. Three days ago, if someone had come up to him asking for money, he'd have laughed in his face, or informed him coyly to get a job. The world, thought Artemus, was finally taking its revenge.

He looked toward the phones again. A man was already using the one on the left—an absolutely despicable looking soul with long hair, shaggy beard, worn out T-shirt, cigarette in one hand and an oversized bottle of beer in the other. He held the phone with his shoulder and spoke dispiritedly to the party on the other end.

Artemus was struck with an idea: what were the chances of finding a quarter in the change slot of that other phone? He'd seen others do it. Why not him? Surely God was aware of his situation. Maybe the heavens had actually arranged for a quarter to be waiting for him. His confidence surged as he reached the phone and thrust his finger into the slot.

Nothing. Nada. No quarter.

He pressed the return lever. The story was the same.

"Need a quarter, kid?"

The man on the other phone drew a final puff on his cigarette, then dug his hand into his pocket. He tossed Artemus the coin. "Merry Christmas."

Artemus caught the quarter with his left hand, keeping the one with the handcuffs hidden inside his shirt. He gaped at the stranger's face. The man turned away, continuing his somber conversation.

"Thank you," said Artemus.

The stranger smiled thinly, then returned to his private world—a world that apparently wasn't running all too smoothly. Artemus had been saved by a man he'd have avoided like the plague in any other circumstance. What was more, the man had saved him despite facing his own personal crisis. Artemus felt the sting of shame.

Still, there was no time to lose. Deliverance was

within his grasp. Artemus dropped the coin into the slot and dialed. An operator came on the line.

"Collect call to this number," Artemus instructed, bouncing nervously on his toes. "From Artemus. No, no! Make that—'From your son, Artie.'"

"Please hold to see if the charges are accepted," said the operator.

If they're accepted? Artemus hadn't even considered the possibility that his call might not be accepted. What if the desk sergeant was right? What if his family didn't want him back? *Impossible!* Of *course* they wanted him back. Of course—

"Answering machine," the operator declared. "Try again later."

"Wait!" cried Artemus. "Can I leave a message?"

"You'll have to deposit an additional—"

"No, *please*! Just a short message! Just ten seconds!"

"Please try your call later."

"*Five* seconds! Don't—"

The line went dead. The operator was gone. Artemus hung up in despair. Where could they be? He retrieved his quarter. The man who'd given it to him was gone. Artemus spotted him climbing into a rusty pickup. *I'm gonna do it*, he thought. *I'm gonna ask him if he has any more change.* But just as he was stepping off the curb, a patrol car pulled

127

up to the gas pump. Artie stiffened. *Hide!* But where? Inside the store!

He slipped inside the AM/PM and made his way to the back corner. The cashier was distracted, reading a magazine. Artemus peered over a potato chip rack. The policeman stepped inside. "Ten dollars on four," he told the clerk. He leaned on the counter as if he were about to glance over the rest of the store.

Artemus turned. He pretended to be getting a soda. His hand trembled as he filled the cup. He continued to hide his handcuffed wrist. The next several seconds were agonizing. Was the policeman watching his back? Had he been recognized?

The bell jingled above the door. The officer had returned to his car.

Artemus waited until the patrol car drove away. *Too close,* he sighed. This whole thing was way too dangerous. He couldn't just stand around, calling collect every five minutes. But what other choice did he have?

The cashier was looking at him suspiciously now. He went back outside. Did the cashier suspect something? Artemus shook himself. *He was driving himself crazy!*

Just then his eyes hit upon a white GMC pickup pulling up to the pumps. The driver wore a cowboy hat and vest. What riveted his focus was the license plate—Utah! The driver was from his home state!

The pickup bed was covered by a blue tarp. A new idea popped into his mind. What if the cowboy was filling his tank for a reason? What if he was heading *home*? Artemus didn't waste time. As the driver went inside to pay, he made his way behind the truck and pulled up one edge of the tarp. Under it was strewn a heap of small cardboard boxes and other supplies. The tarp was secured just tight enough to keep things from bouncing out. After making a final survey of the area, he squeezed under it and found a place along the right wheel well. He realized the truck might simply drive to some location in Las Vegas and park for the night. But how could this leave him any worse off than he already was? And what if he hit the jackpot? What if the driver blazed a trail directly to Salt Lake City? By morning, he might be *home*!

Artemus heard the cab door open and close. The pain in his stomach returned. He had to eat something soon. His strength was fading. As the truck pulled out, he visualized all his favorite meals topped with gravy. He even pretended to chew and swallow. It occurred to him that he'd never told his mother how much he appreciated her cooking—or how he appreciated anything else, for that matter. *I'll tell her the first chance I get,* he promised. *I'll tell everyone how much I miss and appreciate and love and . . .* He swallowed as the thought clumped in his throat.

He was on his way. It wouldn't be long now. For the first time in days, he felt certain he was finally on the road back home.

Fourteen

❧

IT WAS A snowball fight! Every man for himself—or woman, as in the cases of Charlotte and Amber. As Chess mercilessly drove the two girls into the garage, it did not appear that the male-dominated sport of snowball fighting would be seriously contested that day. However, unbeknownst to him, a conspiracy was underfoot. As soon as he allowed himself to become distracted, Amber tackled him from behind while Charlotte grabbed an empty plastic bucket and buried him with snow several times over.

"Uncle!" Chess cried. "Uncle!"

"Where?" asked Amber playfully. "I don't see any uncle!" She then plastered the top of his head with a bucketful of her own.

"I give up, already!"

"Okay, I think he's had enough," said Charlotte, laughing between pants. "Let's get the tree inside. My hands are *freezing*!"

They left a trail of pine needles from the front door to the living room as they carried inside what had been the tallest tree on the lot—almost eleven feet. It was hoisted, majestic and invincible, in the corner where the staircase met the balcony. Charlotte retrieved three dusty boxes from the basement containing a lifetime collection of ornaments and other Christmas knickknacks that she hadn't seen in almost eight years. She unfurled from a bed of newspapers the old white tinsel angel with its curls of long black hair—an heirloom that her grandmother had bestowed on her during her first year of marriage, also the year that her grandmother died. Lovingly, she smoothed some of the ruffles and conceded that it looked as elegant as ever. Her eyes moistened. How could she have allowed such a beautiful thing to sleep in this box for so long? Chess was privileged to place the angel on the pinnacle of the tree by leaning over the balcony. Charlotte and Amber admired the scene from across the room, their arms wrapped about each other's waists.

"Do you think Dad will like it?" Amber inquired.

"Yes," Charlotte replied fondly. "I think he will."

Jordan pulled into the driveway at a quarter to six.

The display that met his eyes reignited a childlike euphoria—the same euphoria he'd felt as a boy when he and his father had hung the first strings of lights along the porch of his old house on 17th South. A similar array of blinking lights now outlined the doorway and the rim of his present house, as well as decorating the hedges along the driveway. Charlotte and the children must have been working nonstop since school let out. Granted, it was a scene repeated in nearly every yard in the neighborhood. But this was *his* yard. *His* house. His enchantment intensified as he stepped through the front door. A lump swelled in his throat as he gazed upon the eleven-foot evergreen and all the other decorations that now festooned his living room. It was Christmas again in the Holiday home. It was really Christmas. And all because one child, his son, had shown the courage to lead the way.

His eyes turned to meet those of his wife. She saw that he was touched, and this touched her all the more. She went to him. They embraced and soaked in the emotion. In their minds they could almost see the face of their little son, beaming a smile of approval from heaven.

Chess was looking down at them from the balcony. "I think I got my accents down," he announced. He then proceeded to recite all six of his lines from the play. To Jordan, the accent sounded rather more Australian than Cockney. But at least he now had his lines flawlessly memorized.

Half an hour later the Holiday family loaded into the car again, eager to deliver Chess to his opening-night performance in *A Christmas Carol* at East-mont High. It was dark as they pulled out of the driveway.

In the interest of making his own contribution to the Christmas spirit, Jordan suggested they might sing some carols. Chess promptly belted out the first verse of "Grandma Got Run Over by a Reindeer." Amber was quick to accompany him.

Jordan smiled and turned to his wife. "Well, it's a start."

He and Charlotte joined in with the chorus as they rounded the corner at the end of the block.

No one noticed the darkened Buick parked by the side of the street. Or the shadow of the man sitting behind the wheel.

Sly as a fox, Boone laughed to himself. *Shrewd as a Southern lawyer.* The kid had style. There was no doubt of that. And spunk! The story of how he'd pulled this off was worthy of a Hollywood screenplay—or at least a training manual for swindlers the world over. *Reminds me of me,* thought Boone, patting himself on the back.

He couldn't wait to hear the details of how Chess

had managed to don the mantle of an upper-class brat and fool a family of complete strangers into accepting him as one of their own. So as the Lexus rounded the corner for destinations unknown, Boone turned on the ignition, spun a U-turn in the frozen street, and followed.

When they pulled into a parking lot next to a local high school, Boone turned in after them, parking just a few rows away. He watched Chess disappear into a rear door after receiving a kiss—*a kiss, no less!*—from the woman who believed she was his mother. Boone stood only three people behind the family as they waited to purchase tickets. He managed to con a free admission by claiming that he wasn't staying for the show, but that he was a father looking for his daughter, and "could he have a quick peek inside?" They surely wouldn't have bought such a line from a teenager, but Boone was whisked right on in.

From the rearmost corner seat in the auditorium's nosebleed section, Boone watched with ever-increasing curiosity as the play unfolded. When, toward the end, Chess emerged from the wings to take center stage below Scrooge's window, he burst out with a knee-slapping guffaw, though no joke had been delivered. *The kid was a genius! An utter genius!*

But for Boone, the celebration had little to do with Chess's newly discovered flair as a stage actor. The kid had fooled everyone! He'd successfully melded himself into a brand new life. He had this Lexus-strutting family eating right out of his palms. For Boone, this meant that the opportunity for plucking this Christmas turkey clean might be better than he could have ever anticipated.

"You were great!" Charlotte told Chess with another kiss after she'd found him backstage.

"Yeah," Chess responded, seemingly distracted.

"You okay?"

He snapped out of it. "Yeah, sure. Thanks, Mom."

As they walked toward the car, Jordan announced, "It's only nine o'clock. What do you say we drive down and see the lights on Temple Square?"

"I think that's a marvelous idea," said Charlotte.

"Oh, we haven't seen the lights in years!" said Amber.

Chess expressed no opinion. His eyes searched the clusters of people making their way to their cars. He'd heard something while he was onstage, and the noise had rattled his nerves. He knew he might be overreacting. There must have been a thousand people in that audience—a thousand voices sending up uncountable bursts of laughter. Was it just his imagination that one of those laughs had sounded strangely familiar?

The Holiday family concluded the day's festivities

with a visit to the city's principal tourist attraction—
the half-million lights that glittered and glowed,
winked and twinkled across the grounds of the
Latter-day Saints' temple. The spectacle covered a
full square block. Every tree was a chandelier and
every hedge a candelabra. And all in the midst of the
hundred-year-old granite temple with its six tow-
ering spires, the highest of them surmounted by a
fire-golden angel.

They parked their car across the street and made
their way inside the gate. The grounds were packed
with spectators, as they always were at this season of
the year. Charlotte and Jordan walked arm in arm.
Amber directed them this way and that, mapping
out what she felt was the best course to stroll down
every walkway.

Chess was finally starting to relax a little. He decided he must have been hearing things. He reminded himself that Boone was gone forever. It
seemed bizarre that only two days ago, this prospect
had frightened him terribly. Now it filled him with
gleeful relief. He'd always convinced himself that
Boone was family, and that any misery was better
than loneliness. He was ready now to draw a new
conclusion. Boone may have been related, but he
was definitely *not* family. "Family" was more than
blood. It was a state of being, a place of refuge, a safe
zone in a world of adventures.

He shuddered as he imagined things returning to the way they were. He knew it couldn't happen. He couldn't have explained why; he just knew it. As he passed before the nativity scene in front of the Visitors' Center, allowing his gaze to come to rest on the infant lying in the manger, an explanation popped into his mind. The answer was reinforced as his eyes climbed the Visitors' Center walls and settled on the white marble monolith of Jesus Christ. The statue seemed to be gazing back at him through the window of the magnificent domed rotunda. Its arms were outstretched in love, ready to welcome all mankind into the *family* of God. *Yes,* thought Chess. The adult image of the ancient Messiah cinched his opinion. It was *He* who had orchestrated this incredible twist of fate. What other explanation was there?

And so the conclusion was undeniable: God was real! And despite looking out for the rotations of the heavens and the blazing of the stars, he'd found the time to rescue little Chess Folsom. True, he may have taken his precious time. But all of that was over now. It was *over*. Chess was the owner of an ultimate gift—a gift that had healed and soothed and saved his soul. And after presenting Chess with such a magnificent present, God could never, *ever* take it away. It wasn't possible. It wasn't logical. It was outside the realm of all—

Chess froze.

His heart stopped. His lungs petrified. Reality came screaming back at the pitch of a braking freight train. There, across the snow-covered lawn, poised calmly behind the ropes on the opposite walkway, stood his Uncle Boone, a grin creasing his cheeks.

Boone opened his hands in a gesture that said, *Are you happy to see me?* Chess shook his head, not so much in reply as in horror. This couldn't be happening. He'd had every confidence, felt every assurance that this could never happen. His old existence, his former life, was gone. It was gone! It was gone! So how could Boone be standing there? *This wasn't happening!*

Chess broke into a run. Boone's grin turned down.

"Artie!" Jordan cried. "Where—?"

The boy didn't stop. He dashed through the north gate, crossing the street, forcing a minivan to slam on its brakes. His family pursued, confused and bewildered.

Jordan found him shivering in the snow beside their locked car, sweating profusely despite the sub-freezing temperature. "What happened, Artie?" he asked, panting. "What's wrong?"

Chess looked up. Up into the eyes of his father. His *father*? How long did he think he could fool himself? This was not his family. He *had* no family. He'd never

139

had one, and he never would. Not even the deepest yearnings of his soul could change the truth.

As tears streamed down the boy's face, Jordan put his arm around Chess's neck. "It's all right," he consoled. "I know what you're feeling. And I understand."

Chess shook his head. "No. You *don't*—"

Jordan looked him in the eye. "I understand better than you think. But everything is going so well. Don't let it slip away. It's taken years to come this far. This is how it's *supposed* to be, Artie. It's Christmas! And nothing from the past will change that. We may grieve, but Christmas will still come every year. Christmas is still first and foremost a day of healing. A day of embracing everything good and wholesome in this world. I never want any of us to ever forget that again. It was *you*, son, who helped me to see it. To bring it back into focus. You were the first. The first to be strong. Now let us be strong for *you.*"

Chess's tears stopped. He looked at Jordan with mesmerized awe. Did he really understand? Was this really the way it was supposed to be? Would he really support him, no matter what? He didn't follow all of what Jordan was saying, but the essence was clear. He would be strong for him. He would *protect* him. Charlotte and Amber had arrived as Jordan was speaking. They'd stood behind him, nodding to everything he said. All of them seemed solidly determined to keep him as part of their family.

Chess wiped his tears and declared, "We have to leave here. We have to go home."

Jordan sympathized. "All right, son. It's getting late, anyway."

Charlotte helped him to stand. She embraced him. Chess looked over her shoulder. The temple grounds were closing. There were hundreds of people exiting the gate. He couldn't see Boone. But he knew he was there, somewhere.

Charlotte rode in back with Chess. She snuggled close, hoping to offer some maternal comfort, but Chess pressed his face to the window, frantic to see if he might spot Boone again. His uncle didn't appear. Chess was half-tempted to believe he hadn't seen him at all. Like the laugh in the auditorium, this too was a figment of his imagination—the afterimage of a former ghost. But he couldn't deny it anymore. This ghost was real. Boone had returned. And his haunting image would appear again soon enough.

Fifteen

❧

S-SO COLD.

In just the last hour, the temperature had plummeted. He should have expected it. But for some reason, as he'd peeked out from beneath the tarp a while back and realized that he was in St. George, Utah, the fear of freezing was the last thing on his mind. Instead, he experienced a rushing elation. He'd been right! The driver of the pickup was heading home. He'd find himself encircled in the arms of his family by morning!

During that brief stop in St. George, as the driver refilled his coffee mug, Artemus took advantage of a sliding rear window on the cab. The cowboy had left a stack of munchies on the seat—a bag of Cool Ranch Doritos, a box of Hostess Twinkies, and a sack of sunflower seeds. Artemus reached inside and nabbed the whole stash. He was safely back under the tarp when the cowboy returned to discover that his entire food supply had been shanghaied. Artemus listened to a colorful string of expletives followed by a shout to some bystanders of, "Hey, did you see anyone come near my pickup?"

A few moments later the truck was back on the interstate, and Artemus was cramming his throat full of Twinkies. It was shortly thereafter, as the pickup began climbing toward the town of Cedar City, that he started shivering. Being in Las Vegas, he'd almost forgotten that it was winter everywhere else in the country—and all he was wearing was a pair of pants, a torn shirt, no shoes, and an ice-cold pair of handcuffs.

If, in fact, this truck was headed to Salt Lake, its destination was still four and a half hours away. *I'll die back here!* thought Artemus. By the time he arrived, all they'd find was a block of ice with him inside. He curled up into a ball and tried to rub heat back into his fingers and toes. After a while this did no good. His shivering became more violent. His flesh was going numb. *I'm not gonna make it,* he admitted to himself.

There was only one option. He was going to have to come out from under the tarp and knock on the pickup's back window. If his surprise appearance didn't inspire a heart attack, he might convince the driver to show him some mercy. Then again, the sight of those handcuffs on his right wrist was sure to raise a suspicious eyebrow. He'd have to hope that the driver wouldn't simply lock the other half around his left wrist and drop him off on the doorstep of the nearest sheriff.

About that time, Artemus realized that the pickup was slowing down. It was pulling off the interstate. He'd been wrong; the driver was *not* going to Salt Lake. He didn't know whether to call this a blessing or a curse. He wouldn't arrive home as soon as he'd imagined, but at least he might not arrive as an ice statue. Then again, there was no guarantee that this trip was nearing an end. For all Artemus knew, the driver would cruise across the countryside for hours. He might freeze to death anyway!

He decided to take a chance and hope that the cowboy's destination was near at hand. It just wasn't worth the risk to come out of hiding. Not if there was any possibility that he might be turned over to the police, shipped off to Florida, and never see his family again.

For another half an hour Artemus endured the bitter cold, thinking only the warmest thoughts: the steam from a cup of hot chocolate . . . sitting with his family around a toasty living room fire . . . the feel of a warm comforter that his mother would pull over his shoulders in the middle of a frozen winter night. . . . He concentrated hard, and wondered if he truly began to taste the chocolate and feel his family's insulating love. The pickup seemed to be winding up the side of a mountain, but then it leveled off and started descending. Shortly thereafter, he felt the crunch of a dirt road under the tires. One final turn, and the truck rolled to a stop.

Artemus remained as still as he could, although he continued to shiver like a bowl of Jell-O. The driver climbed out of the cab. Artemus heard the jingle of keys and then a heavy wood door open and close. After that, everything was quiet, still, and dark.

He lay there for a good ten minutes before he was convinced that nobody was coming back. Apparently the hour was too late for the cowboy to unload his supplies. The air was slightly warmer, and he smelled the strong musks of oil and grease. It was pitch-black as he poked his head out from under the tarp. He sensed that he was inside a garage. Slivers of light outlined the door leading into the main part of the house. His vision started to adjust. The place was a menagerie of tools and old tires, band saws and greasy car parts. The junk peaked higher than the pickup in some places, appearing as if it might spill over on top of him. Artemus marveled that there had been room enough to park at all.

Still shivering, his skin itching from frostbite,

Artemus climbed out of the bed and stood on solid ground. He moved carefully to avoid knocking something over and causing a ruckus, following a pathway between the debris that led to the door. Not that he had any idea what he was going to do when he got there. Perhaps he was hoping to find a current of heat seeping out from between the cracks. The garage might have been warmer than the open air, but it certainly wasn't toasty or comfortable.

While rubbing his goose pimples, he noticed something on a bottom shelf. *Could it be?* As he edged closer, his suspicions were verified. A space heater! That little metal box could be his salvation! That is, if it worked.

He found an outlet above the workbench to his right. With shaking, anxious hands, he plugged the heater in and turned the knob. The coils glowed. Warmth! Precious warmth! *Thank you, God. Thank you.*

Only after he'd finished thawing his hands and feet did he allow himself the luxury of feeling nervous or frightened. And only after he'd snitched a box of ice cream sandwiches and a package of frozen Polish sausages from a corner freezer did he begin to wonder where in the world he'd found himself. Wherever it was, he knew it was still a long way from home. Yet for the moment, he was satisfied just to have the simple commodities of heat and food.

Compared with the rest of his day, the comforts he now enjoyed were fit for a king. The events of tomorrow would come soon enough. For now, he would savor his sausages warmed in front of the heater, and dream of his warm, comfortable bed beneath his familiar canopy of model airplanes. Such a place seemed to exist in some never-world at the moment—a paradise he'd invented in his imagination to hide the bitter reality of the world he now occupied.

He felt to see if the quarter was still in his pocket. At first light, he'd brave the cold and find a pay phone. And yet as the hours wore on, his mouth watered more and more at the prospect that just beyond that door sat a phone that wouldn't cost him anything at all. Even if his parents weren't home, he might still leave a life-saving message without any operators demanding more coins. The temptation to open that door and sneak inside percolated and simmered. *Be patient,* he told himself. A hasty move now might cost him the opportunity forever. He realized that his next effort to restore some semblance of truth and order to his life might be his last.

Sixteen

CHARLOTTE OPENED HER eyes to see that the covers were pulled back on the opposite side of the bed. No head slept on the pillow. She pondered this for a moment, then pulled her robe around her shoulders and made her way down to the dining room.

Jordan was seated at the table, basking in the quiet radiance of the Christmas tree lights. When Charlotte first saw his face, he seemed entranced by the lights, as if his spirit had departed for a moment to another place.

"Honey?" she inquired.

Without the least indication that Jordan had noticed her or even heard her approach, he said, "There was someone there."

Charlotte might have asked him what he was talking about, but she was used to her husband starting a conversation in mid-thought, especially when he had that faraway look. So she merely made her way over to the table and sat beside him.

Jordan looked at her. "That day. That morning. There was a woman."

"A woman?"

"She was on the bridge."

"What bridge?"

"The old wooden bridge a quarter mile down the river. Remember? The one the local farmers use every summer to bring hay down to the river bottom to feed the horses. That morning when . . . it happened . . . I remember I grabbed on to that fallen tree. I wedged myself in the branches. Just before I . . . before I blacked out . . . I remember looking up and seeing . . . a lady standing there. She wore a long white coat and had long black hair. I'd forgotten completely. That is, until this morning, when I was stuck in traffic. I didn't think I'd ever forget a single detail of that day. But I did."

"I don't remember seeing a woman," said Charlotte quietly. "Certainly not one dressed in white, with long black hair."

"You don't?" Jordan considered this. He gazed up

149

at the Christmas tree again. "That's funny. Because I see it so clearly. She was watching me. Just watching. In fact, I think I always wondered if it was her who ran and got help."

Charlotte shook her head. "*I* found you that morning, Jordan. *I* was the one who ran and got help. There was no one else."

"Really?" He continued to watch the lights.

"Is this what's keeping you awake, my love?" she asked. "This memory of something or someone that you saw?"

Jordan smiled uncertainly. "Pretty silly, isn't it? I don't know what it is. I guess it's just . . . I guess it bothers me to think I might forget . . ."

Charlotte turned her eyes to determine exactly what her husband was staring at. It was the heirloom angel atop the Christmas tree, with its long, white robe and black curled hair. Charlotte laid her palm over her husband's hand. "Maybe, Jordan, what you saw was meant to comfort you. A symbol of something else. Something very good."

Jordan sighed. "If so, I can't imagine what it could mean."

She squeezed his hand. "It's late. Almost four o'clock. We should get some sleep."

Jordan nodded.

"It'll all be clearer tomorrow," she assured. "Everything always makes more sense in daylight."

"Yes," said Jordan, rising to let her lead him back. "It always does."

Seventeen

THE ROOSTER HAD crowed well over an hour ago, rousing Artemus from his sleep. But he couldn't bring himself to move. It was still so bitter cold. *Just let the sun rise a little higher,* he told himself. *Let it warm up a few more degrees.* Then finally he might have the courage to venture out into the weather, his feet wrapped in grease-stained rags from the pile that he'd used for bedding.

Artemus had no idea how close he might be to a pay phone. Or even how close he was to a town. Based on what he could see through the garage's ice-crusted window, he was in the middle of nowhere—some sort of a farm or ranch.

His best hope of redemption still rested with the phone inside the house. But how could he sneak inside and dial it without being discovered? He had to do something soon. The cowboy might return to unload his supplies at any moment. He was just about to toss in the towel—knock on the door and hope the cowboy allowed him to call home before phoning the police—when he heard some sort of screen door at the back of the house open and shut.

Artemus stood and looked through the window into the backyard. The cowboy, now bundled in a down jacket and snow boots, was walking away from the house toward a tall, gray barn and an aluminum shed that might have been a chicken coop. Off to do morning chores, or so it appeared.

This was his chance. He couldn't hesitate. But what if the cowboy wasn't the only person living here? He'd heard no other voices. He had to take that chance. He opened the door and slipped inside. The house was *freezing*! This guy must have been part Eskimo!

He passed through a hall with a shelf rack that displayed several pairs of boots and a variety of coats. *Thank heavens!* Artemus slipped the ugliest, grimiest, and (by coincidence) *warmest*-looking of the coats over his shoulders. His arms didn't even come out of the sleeves, but who cared?

As he stepped into the kitchen, he began to sense a rise in temperature. The heat source came from the next room—an old-fashioned wood stove. Artemus

153

began searching desperately for a phone. What if this guy *had* no phone? If he still used a wood stove, maybe he didn't believe in phones, either. No, there *must* be a phone. No one in their right mind would live out here without some means of communication. But *where*?

Bingo! There it was, sitting unpretentiously on a table in the next room, right beside a window that looked out into the backyard. Perfect! If the cowboy returned, he'd see him coming. Artemus grabbed the receiver. His heart rate quickened. He started to dial. *Shoot!* In his anxiousness, he forgot to include the long distance prefix. He tried again. This time he hit the wrong number altogether. He shrieked in exasperation. *Okay, settle down. Settle down.* He drew a deep breath. Then he dialed again.

"Two hundred dollars!" Chess exclaimed.

Amber looked down her nose at him. "What are you complaining about? Isn't that enough?"

She'd entirely misinterpreted his surprise. Chess wasn't disappointed. He was overwhelmed. Two hundred dollars to buy Christmas presents? He and Boone had sometimes lived a full month on two hundred dollars!

"Half of it is your allowance," said Amber. "The other half is a donation from Dad. But if you go off like last year and blow any part of it on arcade games or model airplane parts, don't expect me to cover for you."

Chess shook his head. "I wouldn't dream of it."

"Dad expects us to buy nice things this year— especially for Mom. In fact, we might consider pooling our resources. Let's buy Mom and Dad something really special. Like a glide rocker and an ottoman."

"A what and a what?"

"Furniture, nitwit."

"Don't we got enough furniture?"

Amber rolled her eyes. "Forget it. You get what *you* want, and I'll get what—"

The phone rang. Amber went to it. "—And I'll get what I want. But we better get going. I promised Mom we'd be back by one o'clock." She picked up the receiver. "Hello?"

"Amber?" said the voice. And then with greater exhilaration, "*Amber!* Thank heaven!"

Amber crinkled her nose. "Who is this?"

"It's me! Can't you tell? But I need help, Amber. I don't know where I am. Listen. I can't talk long—"

"Clifford Durfee, is that you?"

"Amber, it's *me*! Your brother! It's Artie!"

She looked at Chess, then directed her attention back to the phone and thinned her eyes. "Clifford, I told you already, I don't like you. I never have liked you, and I never will. Don't you have anything better to do so early on a Saturday morning?"

"Amber, *please*! I'm not Clifford! Let me talk to Dad!"

"Wouldn't you rather talk to yourself?"

"Myself? Amber, what are you—?"

Amber held the phone toward Chess and mouthed, "Say 'Hi, Clifford.' "

Awkwardly, Chess said into the mouthpiece, "Hi, Clifford."

She pulled back the phone. "I'm warning you, Durfee. Don't call here again. I'll have the police trace your line and cut off your phone for good."

"He's coming back! Please, Amber! Let me talk to Dad! He's coming back!"

"You're a fruitcake, Durfee! And you do a lousy impression of my brother! Remember, you've been warned!"

Amber slammed down the phone. She huffed and turned to Chess. "Are all boys that crazy, Artie? Should I be worried?"

Chess didn't hear a word she said. He looked white.

Amber snapped her fingers in front of his face. "Hello? Anybody home?"

"Huh?" said Chess.

Amber gruffed. "That proves it. You *are* all crazy. Let's go."

She headed for the door. Chess stared at the phone. An awful feeling curdled in his stomach. He shook himself, attempting to crush the thought like a burning ember. Finally, he turned briskly and followed Amber out the door.

He was coming back in the house! Artemus dropped the phone onto the table and scrambled back into the kitchen, back into the hallway that led toward the garage.

The cowboy reentered through the rear door, whistling a John Denver tune and stomping the snow off his boots. He held a half-dozen eggs against his chest.

He'd already cracked several eggs into a frying pan by the time he heard an obnoxious tone coming from his phone. That was strange. It was off the hook. He scratched his head a time or two, then decided he must have bumped it on the way out.

An hour later, he discovered the glowing space heater in his garage. This prompted a paranoid inspection of the grounds around the house, but by then Artemus was long gone down the bleak country road. It would be almost a week before the man noticed that an overcoat and an old pair of hiking boots were missing from the hallway off the garage.

Eighteen

THE FANTASY WAS crashing. Crumbling all around him. The crash seemed to reverberate with each step that Chess took down the snowy sidewalk. With every glance he stole to the right or left looking for his uncle's Buick, a noose seemed to tighten around his throat.

It was that phone call! It needled and tormented him. Even if it was a prank call from one of Amber's demented admirers, it had forced him to reface the question he'd been so conveniently ignoring for three days: What had become of the *real* Artemus Holiday?

It all seemed so savagely cruel. How could heaven have allowed him a mocking glimpse of what his life might have been, only to strip it mercilessly away?

He wished he'd never known. He was happier not knowing. *Please God,* he pleaded inwardly. *Don't take it away. Don't take it away.*

"Are you all right?" Amber inquired as they sat on the bench awaiting the bus.

"Sure," said Chess. "I just have a headache."

"You're sweating. What's the matter with you?"

"Nothing," Chess insisted. "I'm just—"

"How come you keep looking back down the street? Are you expecting someone?"

"No, I'm—" Chess drew a deep breath. "I'm fine. Really. I'm fine."

The bus arrived and carried them ten minutes down the road to a small shopping plaza filled with gift and specialty shops. Amber had judged it to be a perfect nook for buying Christmas presents. Chess didn't have the foggiest notion what to purchase. What do you buy for a family that seems to have everything? He pursued only one idea—something for his mother—er, that is, for Charlotte. When he set eyes upon the gift it struck a chord deep down inside him, strange and yet familiar, and it brought a smile to his face. It seemed to him the most appropriate gift in the world for a mother.

The clerk warned him that the item was quite fragile, but Chess insisted that she wrap it anyway. He felt it'd be fine for a day or two. Christmas was only the day after tomorrow. If he could just last that

159

long—if he could just linger inside the cocoon of this fantasy through Christmas—that's all he wanted. Was that asking too much?

The answer came, like a blow to the stomach, the moment he emerged from the shop. Parked in the stall directly in front of the store was Uncle Boone's Buick, its engine running. His uncle's arm was propped against the rim of the open window, fingers tapping.

Chess went rigid. Should he run? He wanted so much to flee. Run away forever. But it was pointless. The dream was over. All attempts to hang on to it now were futile. He was Chess Folsom. He could never hope to be anyone else again.

"Well, well," said Boone. The grin that had creased his mug the night before had been wiped away. His mouth was turned down and his eyes were full of enmity. "Who have we here? Could it possibly be a boy named Chess Folsom? Or is it some stranger? Some high society brat who could use a bashing, just for good measure?"

Chess glanced across the plaza to the antique shop that Amber had entered. She was still inside. Chess turned back, but his eyes were toward the sidewalk. "H-hello, Boone."

Boone raised his eyebrows. "So you know me now, eh? The way you ran away last night, I thought I musta contracted some disfiguring disease that made me impossible to recognize."

"I was surprised, that's all. I didn't—I didn't expect—"

Boone clenched his teeth. "Get in the car."

Chess obeyed automatically, the same way he'd obeyed his uncle for the past eighteen months. As soon as he'd closed the passenger door behind him, Boone walloped him across the face. "The next time you pretend you don't know who I am, I'll break you in half. You understand me, boy?"

Chess cupped his hands over his bleeding nose. Just one more bruise to add to the others on his face. "I didn't mean nothin' by it, Boone. If anyone had seen you and me together, it woulda messed up everything."

"Is that so? What are you so afraid of messin' up? You afraid those lunkheads you're stayin' with are gonna find you out? Afraid you won't have no frilly bed to sleep in tonight? Nobody's mama to tuck you in? If that's what you're afraid of, then you got every reason, boy. 'Cause by this time tomorrow you and me is gonna be a thousand miles from this place."

Chess could feel his heart tearing right down the middle. Spiritlessly, he inquired, "Where we goin', Boone?"

"Mexico. Hawaii. The Bahamas. After tonight, we'll pretty much be able to write our own ticket to anywhere in the world. And it's *you* that's gonna make it happen. Don't you see it, Chess? You land feet first right on top of a pot of gold, and you don't see it?"

Chess looked at his uncle, dread building inside him. "What are you gonna do?"

Boone was tempted to bonk him over the head again to help him see. "What do you *think* we're gonna do! We're gonna take these flakes for everything they got! After tonight, there won't be so much as a loose penny under the couch cushions."

Chess could barely speak the words. "You-you're not gonna hurt nobody, are ya?"

"That's up to you, kid. Obviously you've developed a soft spot for these morons. So I'll tell you what you're gonna do." He produced a program from last night's play. "Says here you're doin' it all over again tonight. That right?"

Chess nodded.

"Mom, Dad, and the girlie goin' to see ya?"

"I don't know," said Chess.

"You see that they do," Boone warned. "Because if there's anybody in that house when I get there at exactly seven o'clock tonight, there ain't gonna be nothin' left of 'em but a greasy stain. This may be the opportunity of a lifetime, Chess. I'm not gonna blow it by leaving witnesses. Now tell me, do these people have a safe?"

Chess shook his head. "I'm not sure."

Boone was flabbergasted. "You mean you been livin' there for three days, and it never occurred to you to ask if they had a safe?"

"What was I 'sposed to do, Boone? Just come right out and ask 'em?"

"That's *exactly* what you better do," said Boone. "And then I want you to find out the combination. Finagle the information any way you can. This oughta be cake compared to what you've pulled off already. I also want you to find out where all the other valuables are. Paintings, jewelry, silverware—everything! I know a fence who'll pay top dollar for whatever we can dig up. After you find this stuff out, I want you to write it down. Tell me where it's all at. Then I want you to leave the information in an envelope under the doormat, along with a key to get inside the house. Are you following all this?"

"Sure. I'm following."

Boone glanced at the neatly wrapped package on Chess's lap. "What do you got there?"

"It's a present. For Mrs. Holiday."

"How'd you buy it? They give you money?"

Chess squirmed. "A-a little."

"Cough it up. Come on." He snapped his fingers impatiently until Chess turned over a wad of bills. Boone was impressed. "There's over a hundred dollars here! They just *gave* this to you?"

163

"It's for Christmas presents, Boone. Please don't take it. I still need to buy a gift for Mr. Holiday and for Amber."

Boone folded the money and stuck it in his pocket. "If they can afford to give a kid over a hundred bucks for Christmas presents, I'm sure there's plenty more where this came from."

"But what—what will I say?"

"You'll think of something. You're a clever kid. I have faith in you. Now get outta here before that girl comes lookin' for you. Remember what I told you. Nobody better be in that house. Got it?"

"I got it," said Chess mournfully.

Boone smiled. He reached into the backseat and grabbed a dirty napkin off the floor. Then he gave it to Chess to wipe the blood off from under his nose. "I knew I could count on you. After that play tonight, I want you to sneak away. Meet me behind the school, back near them Dumpsters. You know where I'm talkin' about?"

"Yeah."

"I'll be waiting for you. We're a team, Chess. You know that, don't you?"

Chess climbed out of the car. "I know it." He started to walk away.

"Hey," said Boone.

Chess turned back.

"Sorry I had to sock you."

"It's all right," said Chess.

"You know I love ya, don't you, kid?"

Chess searched his uncle's eyes. He searched deep. It wasn't there. Finally, he nodded and stared back at the ground. "I know it," he said.

Boone faced forward. He threw the Buick into reverse and backed out of the stall, never glancing back. Chess watched him pull into the street and speed away. He looked up at the bright sun and stared until it hurt. Then he shut his eyes and waited for the afterimage to disappear. The feelings were gone. All the emotions that had once lulled him into thinking he might be part of something larger than himself had dissipated. He was alone again. But it was okay. He knew this feeling well. He'd known it all of his life.

Nineteen

❦

ARTEMUS HAD BEEN walking cross-country through the
barren farm fields for over an hour in oversized boots
that filled with snow every time he traversed a high
drift. At last he reached the state highway and a green
sign that informed him that Panguitch, Utah, was another ten miles down the road. *Panguitch?* Where in
blazes was Panguitch? His heart dropped. Even if Panguitch had been paradise, he'd never make it another
ten miles. And yet he *had* to make it. A new incentive
compelled him. His family was in danger. There was
an imposter living at his house!

He'd figured it all out in stages as he mourned over
the bizarre reception he'd received from his sister on
the phone. Why hadn't it occurred to him sooner? If
that man in the motel had mistaken him for some-

body else, might his parents have made the same mistake? It seemed unfathomable, and yet it was the only explanation. It explained events in Las Vegas. It explained why his parents weren't looking for him. Finally, it explained the strange voice that Amber had put on the line.

He knew who it was. That kid from the store. The creep who'd stolen his clothes! How did he do it? How could he have fooled them so completely? Didn't his sister know her own brother? Didn't his parents know their own son?

Artemus couldn't fathom what the motive might be for such a deception. But whatever it was, he had to stop it. And yet he could feel himself weakening by the minute. The wind ripped right through his oversized coat. Ice crusted in his hair and on his eyelashes. He felt his own forehead several times. He was sure he was burning with fever.

A few moments later, a miracle fell into focus. A trucker across the road had found a spot wide enough to catch some shut-eye. His payload was seven cement cylinders, each about six feet long and three feet in diameter, tied crossways on the trailer. Facing the trucker was another green sign: *Salt Lake City, 247 miles*.

Another gamble, another foolish hope, but Artemus had no better prospects. He crept up close and climbed inside one of the cement cylinders. He buried his head under the collar and pulled his knees to his chest, hoping a passing motorist might think he was a bundle of blankets. Twenty minutes later, the engine started to crank. The wheels started to roll.

Once again, Artemus was in the hands of fate. He had no reason to believe that fate might be any kinder than it had been over the past few days. Still, his heart was glowing with optimism. His joy was irrepressible. Was it just the experience of hearing his sister's voice? Was it simply the knowledge that his family was still there, intact, exactly in the place he would have expected? He knew they were in danger, but he took great comfort just in knowing that he hadn't been forgotten. His parents may have been hoodwinked by a despicable little creep, but when all the smoke had cleared, Artemus would still be their son. There was still a place in this world he could call home. From now on, even if his spirit journeyed to the farthest reaches of the galaxy, his heart would forever remain exactly where it began: encircled in his family's love.

Twenty

❧

"So," said Chess, trying to act nonchalant as he spun a quarter on the table, "what would you say, Dad, is the most valuable thing we own?"

"Each other," Jordan replied as he concentrated on the instruction manual for his video camera. He'd purchased the camera four years earlier, but he'd only used it twice. *This* Christmas, however, he planned to record every event, including his son's performance that evening.

"I mean, really," said Chess. "If we suddenly went broke, what would be the most valuable things in our house?"

"Well, there are a number of things," said Jordan. "The diamond brooch I gave your mother on our tenth

169

anniversary would cover a few mortgage payments. The Hegsted painting in the study. My coins . . ."

"Coins?"

"Sure. You've seen 'em. Frankly, Artie, most of our stuff has far more sentimental value than—"

"Where do you keep the coins? I mean, it's been so long since I've seen them."

"What's all this interest in coins and jewelry?" asked Jordan. "You trying to pawn something to pay off an old gambling debt?"

Chess's face reddened. Fortunately, Jordan kept his attention on the instruction manual. Chess felt nauseous. All the lies were wearing him down. He'd been lying nonstop ever since he'd been cornered by Boone, starting with Amber when she'd inquired how come he'd only bought one present.

"This one's for everybody," Chess had replied.

"That single box cost you two hundred dollars?"

Chess refused to let her examine it, claiming it was far too fragile. He'd even turned his pockets inside out to prove that all the money was gone. Amber remained skeptical and said she couldn't imagine *any* gift she'd want to co-own with her parents.

Now, sitting at the table with Jordan, Chess was afraid he might have to excuse himself at any moment to throw up. He was fully prepared to betray the only people who'd ever given him an ounce of real devotion. But that was insane! What was he thinking? Had he forgotten? It was all a *lie*! A deception! If they'd really known him, did he think they'd have given him a single crumb? Of course not! They'd have probably spit in his face like everyone else.

Still, Chess refused to believe it. The Holidays weren't like that. Although he knew that in a few hours he'd never see any of them again, he was determined never to forget them. He wasn't betraying them; he was *saving* them. Chess knew his uncle. He'd seen what he was capable of doing. If Boone couldn't rob them cleanly while they were out of the house, he'd settle on a method that was far less clean.

"All that stuff is down in the safe," said Jordan. "You know that."

So there *was* a safe. "Oh, yeah," said Chess. "Hey, would you mind if I went down and got it?"

"The coins?"

"Yeah. Just for a minute. I'll bring 'em up here. That way you can supervise."

Jordan shrugged. "Knock yourself out. But don't mess things up. I have all our documents filed just how I like—ordered pandemonium."

"I won't," said Chess. He hesitated for a moment, shifting in his seat. "Umm . . ."

Jordan fiddled with the camera. "What is it?"

"Well, I . . . I'll need the combination."

Jordan looked at him over the rim of his reading glasses. "It's not locked, Artie. It never has been. It's just a fire safe, in case the house burns down or something."

"Ah," said Chess. "I see. Well . . . in that case, maybe later."

Jordan gave him another curious glance.

Charlotte stepped into the room and asked Chess, "Are you ready for tonight?"

"I suppose," he replied. "You all are comin', right?"

An apologetic expression swept over Charlotte's face. "I'm not feeling real swift, Artie. I haven't been sleeping well. Would it be all right if I stayed home? We could all watch your father's video after—"

"No!" Chess snapped. "*Everybody* has to come!"

"What's the problem?" asked Jordan. "*I'll* be there."

"You don't understand," said Chess. "It's important! I thought families were supposed to support each other with things like this!"

Amber chimed in from across the room, "One night is support enough."

Chess folded his arms. "Then I won't go. If everybody in this house isn't there tonight, *I* won't be there either."

"Artie," pleaded Jordan. "Your mother doesn't feel well."

"I won't do it. I'm dead serious."

"It's really that important to you?" asked Charlotte.

"Yes!" Chess exploded. "More important than you'll ever know."

Charlotte relented. "All right, Artie. If it means that much, I'll be there."

Chess pointed at Amber. "Her too."

"No way," she protested.

"Amber," said Jordan, "if it means that much to your brother—"

Amber went ballistic. "Mom! You promised I could go to Michelle's! I told you there was a party! I told you over a *week* ago!"

"What time does it start?" asked Chess.

"Seven-thirty, you little weasel. Please, Mom!"

Too close, thought Chess. His tantrum would have to be more dramatic than hers. "If she's not there, I won't go onstage. I swear it."

"The play gets out a little after nine," said Jordan. "You can be a little late. I thought it was fashionable to be late."

Amber sent Chess the dirtiest, crustiest look imaginable. Chess, however, breathed a sigh of relief.

Stiff, frozen, and burning with fever, Artemus wept with delight as the truck crossed over the summit at Point of the Mountain and began its descent into the Salt Lake valley. "Home," he whispered reverently as he gazed out at the city lights cradled between the eastern mountains and the western hills. The valley was glowing red from the setting sun. Who'd have thought the sight of his home town could have filled him with such ecstasy? If he could have carved in stone a decision never to leave this valley again, he'd have done it then and there.

And yet several minutes later, as the truck switched from Interstate 15 to Interstate 80, continuing east toward Parley's canyon, his mind reeled with panic. The trucker wasn't stopping! Salt Lake wasn't his destination at all! *He was driving right on through!* Artemus might have suspected this when the rig filled up with gas forty miles south in Provo, but everything was going so perfectly. He'd started to believe *nothing* could stop him.

Could he jump? He couldn't believe he was even asking himself this. The freeway was racing below him at sixty-five miles an hour. He'd be squashed like a bug! And yet the temptation wouldn't subside. He was *not* leaving this valley. Not after everything he'd been through. Not after coming so close. Maybe he *wouldn't* be killed. Maybe he'd just break a few bones. It almost seemed worth it. At least he'd be home. He'd be *home*!

The point of no return arrived as he watched the freeway exit closest to his house approach, then fade into the distance. This was it! If he was going to jump, he had to do it now!

Suddenly, the brakes on the truck started to screech. The rig was slowing down. He poked his head out far enough to see what was ahead. Lights were flashing. It was some sort of delay. Furniture had fallen out of the back of someone's pickup, and the police were cleaning it up. Traffic was at a stand-still! Artie's heart did somersaults.

After the truck had rolled to a complete stop, he climbed down from the trailer and planted his boots on the asphalt. Horns started honking, trying to alert the truck driver, but Artemus ignored them. His fever still burning, he tromped back toward the free-way exit. Just another mile or two. Another mile to safety.

Twenty-one

THE CLOCK TICKED closer to the time of Chess's departure. The preparations his uncle had requested were completed. He took a house key from the spare key chain hanging on the refrigerator. In the privacy of the main floor bathroom, he wrote down all the information and stuck it in an envelope. As he licked the seal, a salty tear hit his tongue. His heart felt like a millstone. He dried his eyes with a towel and glanced at himself in the mirror.

Look at you, he said to himself. *Sniveling like a baby.* This wasn't the Chess Folsom he knew. Chess Folsom was always tough as nails; immune to drivel like this. But if that was true, why was there a lump in his throat the size of a basketball? Why did he feel as if he were saying goodbye to the only interstice of happiness he would ever know?

Jordan pounded on the door. "Let's go, Artie! You're gonna be late!"

He composed himself. "Coming."

"Everybody's out in the car."

"Be right there."

As Jordan's footsteps fell away, Chess breathed deeply and clenched his jaw. He could be tough as nails again. He was only three days out of practice. He'd reharden in no time. After that, he'd never let himself go soft again.

The car was running as Chess emerged from the house. He pretended to tie his shoe as he carefully placed the envelope and key under the doormat.

Jordan punched the horn. "Hurry! Come on!"

Chess climbed into the backseat with Amber, who still wasn't talking to him. As Jordan pulled away, Chess kept the house in his vision as long as he could.

Charlotte looked in the backseat and noticed tears pricking at his eyes. "Are you all right?" she asked.

Chess perked up. "Yeah. I'm fine."

"Nervous?"

"Yeah. Nervous."

"I'm surprised. You didn't seem so nervous last night. Are you sure you're okay?"

"I'm sure," said Chess. "I'll be just fine. I always am."

* * *

It was ringing. Two rings. Three rings. *Why wasn't anyone answering?* At last the answering machine came on with Amber's voice saying: *"This is the Holiday residence. No one can come to the phone right now. If you wouldn't mind terribly, please leave a message and we'll call you right back."*

After the tone, Artemus cried, "Mom! Dad! It's Artemus! I'm in Salt Lake—at the Maverick station right off the freeway! The boy who's living with you is an impostor! A criminal! He stole my clothes at Nordstrom! The night of my birthday! We switched places somehow. You have to believe me! It's really me! Your son, Artemus! I'm on my way home! I'll be home in just a few—!"

The line disconnected. Time was up. Artemus dropped the phone. He simply let it hang and walked away. The fever was making him dizzy. And yet he still had at least a mile to walk. It seemed like a light-year. Nevertheless, he trudged on.

Block after block fell in his wake. The Christmas lights on people's lawns started to blur. The street lamps reflecting off ice-coated branches glimmered like spidery kaleidoscopes. Part of the time, he wasn't even sure where he was or how far he still had to go. Only one thought pulsed: *Keep walking. Don't stop. If you sit down now, you'll never get up. Just keep walking.*

In time, the sights started to seem familiar. He knew this street. This was a section of sidewalk his feet had pounded a million times. His house was on the very next block. The realization gave him a final burst of energy. Tears trickled out from the corners of his eyes and froze to his cheek. *Almost there. Just three more houses. Just two more yards. Just one more driveway.*

There it was! The sight was overpowering. Home! He was home!

And what a welcome! Lights glittered everywhere—the hedges, the trees, the rim outlining the front door. If that doorway had been the Pearly Gates themselves, Artemus wouldn't have believed it could look any more beautiful.

More Christmas lights blinked inside. Despite this, the place looked closed for the night. Had everyone gone to bed? How late was it? How long had he been walking? For all he knew, he'd been walking the entire night.

He reached out for the door handle. Locked. He should have known. But Artemus knew the secret place. His father always kept a spare key hidden behind the siding. He retrieved it, placed it in the lock, and turned.

A rush of warm, delicious air wafted over him. He stumbled into the foyer and cried as loud as his hoarse lungs would allow, "Mom! Dad! I'm here! I'm here!"

A shadow lunged from the right. His arms were seized. His wrist—the one with the handcuff dangling—was hoisted behind his back. His other wrist was also seized while the other half of the handcuff was pinched in place.

Too shocked for words, too stunned to know what to feel, Artemus turned to see his attacker. Terror imploded within him. The face from his darkest nightmare had returned!

"Unbelievable," Boone Folsom declared. "You, kid, are the *last* person I expected to walk through that door tonight."

Twenty-two

THE HOLIDAYS' LEXUS pulled around to the backstage door where they would drop off Chess. His mood had seemed to darken even further. He wouldn't make eye contact with anyone. Several more inquiries were made as to whether he felt all right, to which he always nodded, "Yes."

"Break a leg, son," said Jordan. "Make it a Kodak moment."

Chess lingered in the backseat, his heart hammering inside his chest. At last his eyes lifted and met those of Charlotte, then Jordan, and finally Amber.

Charlotte laid her hand on his cheek. "Hey," she consoled. "We're all rooting for you. Just remember what you did last night. Everything will be okay."

The boy's lip started to quiver. Suddenly he wrapped

his arms around Charlotte's neck. It took her by surprise. The position was a bit awkward to return the embrace, but she did the best she could. Chess tried to soak in every drop of love that he could, store it in some deep pocket of his soul for future retrieval. But it wasn't working. What did he expect? He was the ultimate hypocrite—seeking love after betrayal. Had there ever been a lower form of scum?

As suddenly as he'd latched on, Chess let her go and slipped out of the car. He rushed inside. The family watched him disappear.

"He'll be okay," said Jordan. "In two hours it'll all be over."

Behind the door, Chess sank to the floor. It was finished. He'd never see them again. Easy come, easy go. Fresh tears rushed down his cheeks.

A fellow cast member spotted him from up the hall. "Artie, come on. They're looking for you." Chess stood. The cast member disappeared into the makeup room.

I can't do it, Chess told himself. *I can't go through with this.* The facade was over. Why drag out the pain? There was no way he was going onstage. No way he could pretend any longer. He was getting out of here. He was going back to meet Boone at the house. He knew the way. If he ran, he might get there in fifteen or twenty minutes.

Chess opened the exit door. After making certain

that the Holidays' car was gone, he fled into the night.

The Holidays took their usual seat in the auditorium. As Jordan pulled his video camera out of its case, his daughter turned to him. "Dad, I need to go use the rest room."

Jordan looked into the viewfinder to check his camera's battery power. "You know where it is?"

"Yes, Dad," she droned and scooted out to the aisle.

Charlotte couldn't seem to relax. She asked her husband, "Do you think I should go backstage and make sure he's okay?"

"He's fine," said Jordan. "Just a bad case of the jitters."

Charlotte continued to fidget. The crowd filtered in and filled up the seats. Charlotte noticed Mrs. Svetson peek through the curtains several times. The last time she seemed to look right at her and her husband, but then the curtains briskly shut and she disappeared.

Jordan checked his watch. The lights should have dimmed five minutes ago. The play should have started.

"Where's Amber?" Jordan asked.

"I don't know," said Charlotte.

"If that girl snuck out of here to go to that party . . ."

"I'd better check on her."

As Charlotte arose, she noticed Mrs. Svetson at the end of the aisle, trying frantically to get their attention. She cupped her hands and mouthed, "Where's Artie?"

Charlotte and Jordan looked at each other with grave concern.

Twenty-three

CHESS WAS BREATHLESS as he raced down the sidewalk to the Holidays' front door. He'd seen his uncle's Buick parked unassumingly beneath some trees across the street, so he knew Boone was inside. He was surprised to find the door slightly ajar; he'd have thought his uncle would have been more discreet. As he stepped into the foyer, he found a pistol aimed right between his eyes.

"Boone! It's me!"

"Chess? What are you doing here? I thought I told you to meet me at those Dumpsters!"

"I cut out early, Boone. I couldn't stick around. We gotta hurry. That play'll be startin' soon. They'll figure out I'm gone."

Boone stepped forward, ready to pummel him

into the carpet. "You lamebrain idiot moron! I told you to finish out the play! Now they'll come lookin' for you!"

Chess noticed several pillowcases filled with valuables gathered on the dining room table. "Aren't you finished here?"

"Not quite. We got one more glitch." Boone stuck his gun back into his coat and nodded toward the living room. The glow of the Christmas tree illuminated someone lying face-up on the couch, their hands pinched behind their back. Chess stepped a little closer.

"Never mind him," Boone gruffed. "Gather up all these pillowcases."

Chess didn't hear him. He continued into the living room. As he drew closer, he recognized the person's face immediately. It was him. The missing piece of the puzzle. The boy whose life he had borrowed for the last three days looked up at him, eyes glazed. Chess wondered if he'd ever seen someone look so helpless and lost. Was this the boy who everyone loved so much?

"Please," said Artemus, his voice weak and hoarse. "Help me."

"He's sick," Chess said to Boone. "What's wrong with him? Where did he come from?"

"None of this is important!" Boone blustered. "Now you get this stuff out to the car, and stay there."

Chess wouldn't move. "What are you gonna do to him, Boone?"

"That's not your problem. That's *my* problem."

He persisted. "What are you gonna do to him?"

Boone seized Chess by the collar with his black leather gloves. He lifted him off his feet and slammed him against the wall, knocking down a picture and shattering the glass. "I said that's not your problem! Don't you hear good, boy?"

Boone's eyes were blazing. Chess had never seen him exhibit such fury. At least, not for a long time. Not since that night. The night of flames. He let Chess slide down the wall until he could stand.

Chess's pleading turned to blubbering. "Please, Boone. Please don't hurt him."

"I told you, Chess. No one's ever gonna know we were here. *No one!*"

"We could t-take him with us," said Chess, his voice a peep. "We c-could get them to pay a ransom—"

"Too complicated. He's already seen us. It wouldn't be *clean*! What's the best con, Chess? You remember?"

Chess was too upset to answer.

"The best con is when the mark doesn't know he's been conned! The best crime has no witnesses. That's how I work. You know that. Now do as I asked ya! Can't you ever do anything the first time I ask?"

Beyond all prudence and reason, Chess continued

pleading, "I've done everything you ever asked, Boone. Things nobody should ever be asked to do. I did 'em 'cause you were my uncle. My only family. Now I'm *begging* you, Boone, *please—*"

Boone laughed caustically. "Don't give me that uncle-nephew-family slop. We ain't blood, kid. We never was. If you're my sister's kid, then I'm the prince of England. She was nothing but a drugged-out piece a trash. She pulled into the driveway one day with a new doll in the backseat. That's all you was, boy. A toy to a half-crazed junkie!"

Chess was flabbergasted. "What are you—? I don't under—"

"I didn't say nothin, 'cause she was almost dead anyway," Boone continued. "When she finally OD'd, we just turned you over to the cops. Now you know! So you listen up, boy, 'cause I ain't gonna ask you again. Either you get that stuff out to the car, or I swear after I torch this place they'll find *both* of you lying in the ashes!"

Chess was trembling so severely he could hardly speak, yet he whispered one more time, "Don't do it, Boone. Don't do it."

That was it. Boone hurled him toward the table. Chess toppled over several chairs and hit his head on the corner. He remained on the floor, half-conscious, groaning.

Artemus, in a state of near-delirium, watched it all from the couch. Boone turned away from Chess and cemented his gaze on to him. Artemus pulled against the handcuffs. It was useless. Even without the cuffs, the fever had drained him of all energy. His only cognizant emotion was panic, horrible and suffocating.

Boone drew near until he stood directly over him. Artemus could see the sweat streaming off his brow, the maniacal look in his eyes. "Please," said Artemus weakly. "Oh, please . . ."

Boone reached for one of the large pillows from the corner of the couch. He gripped it in both hands. Then he began to lower it slowly toward the boy's face.

Artemus tried to scream. The pillow pressed down hard, muffling all sound before Artemus had even drawn a final breath. The struggle was over! The end had come!

Suddenly the pressure went limp. The pillow fell away. Artemus gasped for air and tried to focus his eyes. As soon as he could see again, he realized that Boone was spread out cold on the living room carpet. Standing over him was the boy who'd stolen his clothes. Gripped in Chess's hands was one of the stuffed pillowcases from the dining room table. As Chess heaved the pillowcase back over his shoulder,

Artemus could hear the clank of coins inside. The man who'd tried to kill him had been rendered unconscious by his father's coin collection.

Twenty-four

🌿

As CHARLOTTE AND Jordan pulled up to the house, they were shocked to find the place surrounded by police cars and ambulances. Their nerves were already frazzled from spending the last hour searching in vain for two missing children. Mrs. Svetson had thrown up her hands and decided to let a young actor playing one of Bob Cratchit's children read Artie's lines.

They tried frantically to guess what possible disaster had inspired such a scene. As Jordan jumped out of the car, his daughter emerged from the house and rushed through a gauntlet of onlookers. Her expression utterly distraught, she threw her arms around his neck. "Dad! We tried to call the school! I sent one of the policemen back to look for you, but—!"

"Slow down, Amber! What's going on?"

"I called Michelle to come get me for the party. I'm sorry, Dad. I came back here to change clothes. When I went up to the door, I heard voices. I ran next door to call the police—"

"Where's Artie? Is he here? Is he all right?"

Amber nodded. "He's here. He's inside. But it's not Artie, Dad. I mean, it *is* Artie. But it's not the person who—oh, Dad, I don't know how to explain it."

Charlotte was already on her way into the house. Jordan and Amber followed. A policeman asked Charlotte if she was the mother. She didn't bother to answer and pushed him aside, entering the living room where paramedics had gathered around a boy on the couch. Artie!

Then Charlotte stopped in her tracks. Was it Artie? Yes, of *course* it was Artie! But if this was Artie, then who—?

The boy on the couch reached out to them. "Mom! Dad!"

Jordan and Charlotte went to him. Charlotte held his face against her cheek as she burst into tears. "He's burning up!"

"According to his story, he may be suffering from exposure and exhaustion," said one of the paramedics.

"Exposure and exhaustion? *What in blazes is going on?*"

The policeman tried to explain. "You've had a break-in. An attempted burglary. Apparently you've had a boy living in your house the past several days, falsely claiming to be your son—"

"Falsely claiming—! What are you talking about?"

"It's true, Dad," said Amber. "He looks just like him. But it's not Artie."

The policeman continued. "We've arrested both suspects—"

"Who?" Jordan demanded. "Where?"

"They've been taken into custody. I think the adult male is already in transit."

"What about the boy?" demanded Jordan. "I want to see the boy!"

"Mr. Holiday, I wouldn't recommend—"

Jordan pushed past him. He burst outside onto the lawn and searched until he found the patrol car with an eleven-year-old boy in the backseat. Jordan met the boy's eyes. He stopped short and let the child's pitiable gaze sink down deep into his soul until it pierced something obscure and indefinable. Jordan shook his head in disbelief. *"No,"* he whispered. *"It's not possible—"*

Suddenly a desperate determination welled up inside him. The police couldn't take him. They couldn't have him. But as Jordan took his next lunging step, the patrol car began to pull away. At the same instant, two policemen stepped around from either side and held him back. "Settle down, Mr. Holiday," one of them said. "He's not your problem anymore. He's the problem of the juvenile justice system."

"Can't I even talk to him?" pleaded Jordan.

"Let the officers process him, and I'm sure you can talk to him later. Tomorrow, perhaps."

"But—!" Jordan realized he was shaking. Panic vibrated through every part of his body. The officers released him. He staggered forward to watch the taillights of the patrol car fade into the distance. "I don't understand," he muttered. "I don't understand."

The officers didn't understand either. They had no idea what emotions had suddenly afflicted Jordan Holiday.

The trouble was, neither did Jordan.

Twenty-five

❦

CHARLOTTE CONTINUED TO hold her son's hand in the recovery room at St. Mark's hospital. He'd been asleep now for over an hour. His features looked peaceful and content. And yet, gazing into Artie's face only racked her soul with the most terrible pangs of a mother's guilt. He might have died! She might have never seen him again! How could she not have realized? So many hints. So many red flags. She'd ignored them all. In retrospect, it was so clear. And yet for three entire days she'd gazed into the eyes of someone else's child, and—

Her hands started trembling. Each time she allowed her mind to flash through the events of the past three days, she was besieged by the oddest combination of emotions she'd ever experienced—rage, wonder, confusion, horror, and a visceral depression that pressed so hard she could feel it as a genuine physical hurt every time she breathed.

Jordan was nearby, pacing the hospital room like an animal in a cage. Every time he tried to sit, his nerves prompted him to stand again. They'd both been awake the entire night. Both of them were exhausted beyond description. Amber had fallen asleep in a TV room across the hall.

The sky was pink outside the hospital window. It was Sunday morning. Tonight was Christmas Eve—a far cry from the Christmas Eve they'd been anticipating. For two days they'd believed the sanctity and joy of Christmas had been reborn, resurrected after lying dormant for eight long years. The person they both knew had been responsible now sat in uncertain misery in Salt Lake's juvenile detention center. As Jordan considered this, fresh tremors of anxiety were unleashed in his mind.

He met his wife's gaze. He could tell that she was dying to know what he was thinking. He yearned to hear her thoughts as well, but neither of them had mustered the courage to broach the subject that had been eating them alive since eight o'clock last night.

Finally, Charlotte couldn't take any more. "How is it possible," she started, "that a stranger—a child from a whole different environment—could look so much like . . . ?" The words stuck in her throat.

Jordan closed his eyes, shaking his head. "I don't know, Charlotte. I don't know. These last few days are like . . . a blur to me now. Nothing makes sense. And yet . . ."

Charlotte raised her eyebrows. "And yet what?"

Jordan wasn't sure what he was about to say. He shook his head again. "I don't know."

The hospital released Artemus shortly after sunrise. His fever had broken. The doctor advised plenty of rest. He offered the same prescription to the rest of the family.

As soon as they arrived home, Artemus was put to bed. He immediately faded into a deep, dreamless slumber, nestled soundly in parental security. When he finally cracked open his eyes an unfathomable number of hours later, the first thing he noticed was his father, lounged in the armchair right off the door, his chin resting on his chest, fast asleep. Artemus smiled. That's just where he might have expected his father to be.

The digital clock on his dresser read 11:35 A.M. He'd only been asleep five or six hours, yet it amazed him how much energy he had. How *alive* he felt.

He climbed out from under the blankets. It was snowing outside his window. The gray day mellowed his mood slightly. Foggy memories of the past four days returned. He thought of the boy—the rival he'd first laid eyes upon next to that mirror at Nordstrom Rack—the one who had deceived his family. The one who had saved his life.

On the floor, he noticed the pair of trousers Chess had stolen from him that day, now lying in a crumpled heap beside the closet. On impulse, he crossed the room to check the pockets, wondering if anything was missing or stolen. It was all there: His wallet. His Utah Jazz cards. His picture of Candee Reynolds—all undisturbed. Suddenly he felt intensely ashamed. Was there really anything he owned that he wouldn't have parted with in an instant out of gratitude for what Chess had done?

He stuffed the wallet back into the front pocket. As he did so, his fingers brushed something. There was something else in the pocket. He pulled out a small piece of folded cardstock. As he unfolded it, he realized it was a photograph—*three* photographs, sitting one on top of the other. He studied the images of two people framed in the three separate squares, growing steadily more perplexed.

Jordan stirred and opened his eyes. "Hey," he said to his son warmly. Artemus was still gaping at the photographs. Jordan continued, "You're looking much—"

"Dad," Artemus interrupted, approaching his father. "Who is this?"

"Who is who?" asked Jordan, putting his arm around his son.

He displayed the picture. "This," said Artemus. "The boy is . . . me, right? . . . But who's the lady?"

Jordan glanced at the photographs. He did a double take. His hand snatched the photos from his son. With ever widening eyes, he drew them closer to his face.

Artemus figured it out. "I get it. It's not me. It's *him*, isn't it? Even back then he . . ."

He noticed that his father's face had paled. Jordan was hyperventilating. "Dad?" He feared his father was having a heart attack. "Dad!"

Jordan bolted for the door. He stormed down the hallway and burst into the master bedroom. Charlotte was in the middle of an agonized slumber when her husband's shrieks drew her to full alert.

"Charlotte!" Jordan cried, shaking the photographs. "It's her!"

"Who?"

"The woman in white! The woman with long dark hair!"

Charlotte shook her head, still disconcerted.

"Don't you see? It's the woman I saw on the bridge! I *know* it is! I *know* it!"

Charlotte looked at him in disbelief. She'd never seen him exhibit a more serious expression. "What are you saying?" she gasped.

"I'm saying get your shoes on. We're driving down to juvenile detention *right now*!"

The Lexus flew down the interstate, on its way to the Salt Lake detention center on 7th West. Charlotte remained in a daze. "It's been eight years," she declared. "How could you possibly remember . . . ?"

"It's *her*," Jordan repeated adamantly. "I've never been so certain of anything in all my life."

"It doesn't make sense. What does it mean? I don't understand *any* of this."

"Neither do I," said Jordan. "But *he'll* know. *He'll* know."

She stared again at the dog-eared photographs on the dashboard. The woman with long black hair. The blue-eyed boy. The sight of him caused her heart rate to quicken. It was *crazy*! This whole thing was insane! What did her husband expect to happen? What did he expect the boy to say? What was he trying to prove?

When they arrived a few minutes later, the detention center was closed, which wasn't surprising on a Sunday, the day before Christmas. Jordan had anticipated this. In fact, he'd anticipated every obstacle known to man. Nothing would deter him. He drove around back, past all the signs that warned against non-police vehicles entering the area, and found an intercom situated outside a rear doorway.

Jordan snatched the photographs off the dashboard and climbed out of the car. Charlotte waited, her heart still pounding, as Jordan pressed the intercom button.

"Yes?" said the intercom.

"I'm here to speak with Chess Folsom. He's one of your . . . well, inmates. He was brought in last night."

"This entrance is for police only. Office hours are eight to five, Monday through—"

"I know that. I know that," said Jordan. "I'm begging you to make an exception. I desperately need to talk to him."

"Are you a relative?"

Jordan faltered. How should he reply? That was easy. He'd say whatever might get him inside. "Yes."

" 'Chess' Folsom? Do you mean *Lawrence* Folsom?"

"If he's an eleven-year-old boy, yes! Yes!"

After a pause, the intercom said, "Hold on."

The intercom went silent. After an excruciating moment, an officer emerged from the building. Charlotte climbed out of the car.

"If you want Lawrence Folsom," said the officer, "I can't help you."

Jordan became emphatic. "All I want is five minutes. Just five—"

The officer was shaking his head. "You don't understand. Lawrence is gone. He left for the airport

201

at 11:00 this morning. By now, he's on his way back to Florida."

The wind was knocked from Jordan's chest. *"What?"*

"An investigator from Jacksonville, Florida, flew in to get him this morning. I guess they've had the boy in custody before. The Florida D.A. wasn't taking any more chances. We were told the boy is a material witness in an arson fire that killed two people fourteen months ago. The primary suspect is the boy's uncle. But we were told the kid was an orphan. If we'd known there were any relatives in the area . . . Are you *closely* related?"

Jordan shook his head dejectedly, his mind still reeling. Charlotte studied him in dismay, feeling his pain, her own thoughts still a blizzard of confusion.

They drove away from the detention center in despair. Jordan cursed himself. What did he think he was doing? Was he losing his mind? His eyes turned back to the photographs on the dashboard. The woman. The boy. The image had burned a scar on his retina. What did it mean? What could it possibly mean?

Charlotte realized they had missed their exit on the freeway. She looked at her husband. His face was rigid with determination. He hadn't missed the exit. He'd selected another destination. She didn't ask, and soon she regretted it.

They drove to the south end of the valley. Charlotte's heart skipped a beat as they took the exit at 126th South. She knew the exit all too well. As the two-lane highway descended into the river bottoms, Jordan located the old access road, defined now by a single pair of tire tracks in the snow from some local resident's pickup. He slowed the car to make the turn.

"Jordan," Charlotte pleaded. "Please, no. Why are you doing this?"

"I have to do it, Charlotte. I have to see it."

Every nerve in her body tensed. She braced herself as the Lexus started awkwardly down the uneven road, covered by six inches of snow. The car rocked and jolted as it made its way toward the old wooden bridge. Charlotte was at her wits' end. On the hill above them still stood the old house. She closed her eyes. She didn't want to see anymore. How could he have brought them here? What could have possibly possessed him?

At the edge of the bridge, Jordan parked. He snatched up the picture and pushed open the door, staggering through the snow to the center of the bridge. The images of that horrible day flashed in his mind like a strobe: his little son sinking under the ice, the echo of his own screams, the freezing water seeping into his marrow. The unquenchable grief. The inconsolable agony. And finally, the woman on the bridge, the lady in white with long black hair. The lady in the photographs.

Charlotte was certain her husband had lost it. She opened the door and sank her shoes into the snow-drift, following an uncertain spousal instinct to save him. He stood at the railing, gazing out across the flowing river. "Jordan, my love, *please,*" she begged, weeping.

"It was right here," he proclaimed, checking it against the photographs. "She stood right here! I remember the car, too. A beige hatchback, parked exactly where our car is parked. She was *here*, Charlotte. I'm not crazy. I know what I saw."

Charlotte erupted like a volcano. "What does it matter? What does it matter who or when or what you saw? Andrew is dead, Jordan! My son is *dead*! They found his body. They showed us his coat. Every month I've laid a white gardenia on his grave. We buried him, Jordan. We *buried* him."

Jordan gaped at his wife, speechless, broken. His legs felt weak. He dropped to his knees, clutching the posts of the steel cross-rails. Charlotte went to him. "He's gone," she said unremittingly. "He's gone."

Jordan leaned his face between the rails, staring down at the steady current. Tearfully, Charlotte wrapped her arm around his head, oblivious to the snow and cold.

"Then why?" uttered Jordan softly. "Why did it all happen? The last four days—why?"

Charlotte shook her head in anguish. "Who could ever know? Why does *anything* happen?"

Jordan considered this for a long moment, then he said assuredly, "For a reason, my love . . . and God knows."

Charlotte let this settle in, unsure how to respond.

Jordan continued, "What more do we need, Charlotte?"

She was stymied. "I don't understand."

"What more do we need . . . to convince us? To convince . . . *you*?"

Charlotte leaned away from him, her eyes wide and her mouth hanging open in disbelief.

"If there was an angel present that Christmas," Jordan pursued, "it wasn't the woman on the bridge. She was *real*. If there was an angel . . . an apparition . . . an illusion, it was the child we laid to rest in that cemetery."

Charlotte backed away. Her nerves had frayed. She couldn't take it anymore. Why was he torturing her? Stumbling, she returned to the car and collapsed into the seat, burying her face in her hands.

Jordan anguished for his wife. He knew his blind inferences were tearing her apart. If he was wrong, it was unforgivable. Unpardonable. One last time, he turned his gaze toward the water, flowing ceaselessly under the bridge, billions and trillions of eternal droplets. Such were also the odds. A billion to one. A *trillion* to one. Why couldn't he let it go? Why did he insist on clinging to such a manic denial of things seen and known? Was it worth his wife's sanity? Was it worth his own?

Jordan dragged himself back to the car. Charlotte couldn't even bear to look at him. They drove home in oppressive silence.

The children watched them pull into the driveway. Artemus, feeling much better, had made a bed for himself on the living room couch. Nursing an incomprehensible optimism, he and his sister had kindled a fire in the fireplace and ignited the lights on the Christmas tree. But one look at their parents told them that a veil of impenetrable gloom was about to settle over their home.

Jordan and Charlotte said nothing as they walked through the door. The children hung back, suppressing their need for immediate explanations. Jordan tried to reach out to his wife, but she retreated into the kitchen, desperate to occupy her mind with dishes, preparing a meal—*anything* to keep herself from plunging into an impending breakdown. Jordan dropped into a dining room chair, vexed and exhausted to the point of numbness.

Artemus approached. "What . . . what happened?" he tentatively inquired.

"He's gone," said Jordan absently.

"Gone? Gone where?"

Jordan shook his head. "I'm not sure."

Charlotte began removing bowls and utensils from various cupboards and drawers, far more items than she might have needed for any meal. Jordan watched her helplessly. He knew there was nothing he could do or say. The children knew it, too. They'd seen their mother like this before.

Charlotte opened the refrigerator door. As she reached for the milk, she paused. Something on a lower shelf caught her eye. Puzzled, she leaned down and removed from the back a small, neatly wrapped package with dark red paper and a green ribbon.

She turned around slowly, her eyes fixed upon the object in her hands. Jordan noticed the change in her expression. The children noticed as well. Then they saw the package.

"It's his," said Amber. "It's the present he bought."

"He put it in the refrigerator?" asked Jordan, perplexed.

Amber shrugged. "I guess so. He said it was for all of us."

A shiver caught Charlotte unexpectedly. Jordan arose, Artemus and Amber followed him into the kitchen. The family gathered around as Charlotte laid the box carefully on the counter. She met Jordan's gaze, as if inviting him to open it. He refused with a mild shake of the head. Whatever was in there, he felt instinctively that it was hers to discover.

Charlotte carefully slipped the ribbon off the box, then she picked at one corner, pulling up the paper precisely where the Scotch tape was attached, leaving hardly a rip. She did the same for the other side. At last, she grabbed the final layer and tore it away, exposing the contents for all to see.

For a long moment, no one moved. No one breathed. They waited until the sight could fully settle upon their minds and hearts. Inside was a transparent plastic container with five glistening white gardenias, pure as snow, perfect as the moment they were bloomed.

Artemus looked at his parents in consternation. "How did he know? How could he have known that these were Andrew's favorite—?"

As he met his parents' gaze, the vision of what Jordan and Charlotte could no longer deny penetrated deeply into his soul. Artemus realized that a portion of his heart—a piece that had been severed and forgotten when he was three years old—was glowing warm again inside his chest.

The final feather of conviction had weighted the balance. For Charlotte, nothing more was required.

The shouts of a million voices resounded: their son was alive! He was alive!

And somewhere in the echoes of time and space replayed the images of a forgotten moment—a moment on a bridge eight years before. And a woman in a long white coat. She sat in silence that cold Christmas morning, the tortured mistress of her own illusions and delusions, her long black hair spilled raggedly about her shoulders. In her arms she cradled a bundle of blankets. Inside the bundle lay a small child, lifeless and cold. The child's spirit had departed its frame the previous night, but still the mother held it. She blamed herself, but the child had not abandoned its mortal state because of any mistreatment or neglect. After living for three and a half years in constant pain and physical affliction, it had found a release that had come wholly by natural causes. As a result of the mother's enslavement to mind-ravaging drugs, the child had come into the world with far more disadvantages than most, suffering from an imperfect mind as well as imperfect organs, a constant reminder to the mother of her own crimes and sins. And yet she had loved the child, insofar as she was able. But her love was not enough to free her from her enslavements. Her drug use only intensified after the child's birth. And at the time of his death, during a road trip home to Florida, her perception of reality had fully degenerated, twisted, and blurred.

Ravaged by paranoia, she was certain that if the child's body were discovered, they would lock her away forever, seal her inside a dungeon of darkness from which she would never escape. And so, in her dementia, she determined to provide the child with a grave of her own making—the solitary and tranquil waters of a Utah river.

She sat in her car that Christmas morning at the edge of the bridge, rocking her child in anguish, cursing the stars of heaven for ever breathing life into her soul. But as she prepared to commit the child to the icy waters, a sudden commotion drew her attention. A short distance up the river, a man was flailing his arms in the current. She climbed out of her car and walked out onto the bridge in time to see him caught up in the branches of a fallen tree. What crimes and sins must he have committed to have found himself in such a dire predicament? Surely this was not something in which she had the right to interfere.

And then something far more extraordinary caught her eye. In the shallow waters along the snowy bank below lay the body of a small boy. She wondered for a moment if she was seeing some sort of hallucination, a visionary aftermath of the act she was about to commit. Then she gasped. There was movement! The child was alive!

She scrambled to the water's edge, recovered the limp, half-frozen body, and carried him breathlessly to her car. With the heater on high, she held him tightly inside her coat as the body of her own child continued to lie in a bundle of blankets on the seat beside her.

Live! she cried in her heart. *Oh, please live. I can no longer save my own son, but perhaps ... perhaps ...*

She perceived shallow breathing in the child's lungs. Could it be possible? Had the stars of heaven decreed that the soul of her child should be delivered back to her? Might she have been granted a second chance? Yes! Yes, it was clear! And like her first son, this one would also be named Lawrence.

And so the following March, as the grief-stricken parents of Andrew Holiday were asked to identify their child's remains, they satisfied themselves to view only the mud-encrusted leather jacket that Andrew had worn on that fateful morning—a garment that a deeply disturbed woman had exchanged in a final, desperate effort to cover her tracks.

The exact details of how the Holidays' son had been stripped from their lives would never be known. The woman who had claimed him from the icy river now lay buried beneath the soil of a public plot in a cemetery near Tallahassee, Florida. For the boy she had rescued, the clarity of memory had been forever obscured by the trauma of it all. But such details no longer mattered.

Yes, the odds had been one in a billion. One in a trillion. But what were odds against the hand of God? The same odds might have been laid by any mortal man against the redeeming mission of that tiny infant born on a cold and lonely night two thousand years ago, an infant child fated to one day sacrifice all he had in hopes of reuniting us all, the lost and bereft souls of the world, with the Father of Eternity.

Jordan phoned his attorney, on vacation in San Diego, and demanded that he find out where in Florida his son had been taken and immediately start an investigation that would confirm the truth. As the sun was setting that Christmas Eve, the Holiday family found themselves in the last available seats on a Delta jet bound for Florida. At sunrise on Christmas morning, their rental car arrived at the front gates of the Duval County youth detention facility in Jacksonville.

They clustered together in the visitors' area, eagerly awaiting Chess's appearance at the end of the long, dark hallway. Their hearts pounded with anticipation. At last a door opened, and a shadow emerged. His steps were uncertain. His eyes were

212

blinking as he entered the room, as if he'd just come forth from a dreary darkness and stepped into a marvelous light. As his vision settled upon the smiling, tearful family in the center of the room, his face filled with wonder and trepidation. What were they doing here? Had they traveled all this way to unleash upon him a storm of anger?

"I don't understand," Chess ventured softly. "Why did you come?"

"We came for you," said Jordan. "To be with you at Christmas."

"I thought—" His voice choked up. "I thought you'd never want to see me again."

Jordan's heart laughed at the irony. "Oh, no, Chess," he said, fighting a last great onrush of emotion. "It's already been far, far too long."

Charlotte approached him, gazing deeply into his pale blue eyes. At that instant the years folded together, and between this moment and the last moment when she had looked lovingly into the eyes of her three-year-old boy, it was as if not a single second had elapsed. She wrapped her arms inextricably around her son.

When Artemus was given his chance to embrace his brother, he finally saw in Chess's countenance the clear image of a friend with whom he'd once romped and played and discovered the world—a

213

world that once again they would have the chance to set out and conquer together.

Chess realized by degrees that his life was about to change forever. As the reality finally set in, his eyes welled up with inexhaustible tears. The dream he'd no longer dared to dream had finally come true.

Many knots and tangles remained in Chess's life, but his father, his mother, his brother, and his sister would be there at his side to help unravel every inch and straighten every coil. Eventually a series of tests and testimonies would verify the facts—but for the moment, nothing else was required to celebrate one of the most remarkable Christmas reunions ever conceived.

No matter how the journey of life would unfold for the family of Jordan and Charlotte Holiday, the spirit of Christmas would remain forever constant, representing what it should have represented from the beginning: Hope in the face of despair. Life in the face of death. And light in the face of impenetrable darkness. From now on, every Christmas morning would begin with a glorious sunrise. And every Christmas Day would be accompanied by a song on the wind that spoke of things more beautiful than the eye could see and more wonderful than the ear could hear.

And for Andrew Chess Holiday would resonate the most infinite conviction of all: that tirelessly steering it all from his magnificent throne was the Great Navigator, the Father of heaven and earth, eagerly waiting for that next moment in time when he might scatter his rainstorm of miracles.

If you enjoyed *A Return to Christmas*, don't miss . . .

ANGELS WE HAVE HEARD ON HIGH

by Joan Wester Anderson

In this beautiful book, New York Times bestselling author Joan Wester Anderson gathers together inspiring true stories of the blessings we receive when we least expect them—a joyful reminder of the timeless power of miracles.

Prayers from people far away bring a long-lost son home. The music of Christmas transforms an irritable Santa Claus line at a mall. A cross glows without electricity in a message of hope, and an angel warms a freezing child. All these and other wonderful stories reveal that when we have faith, we find ourselves unexpectedly blessed, every day of the year.